Learn Thru Play:

Creative Activities That Build Attention, Curiosity, and Collaboration

By Carol Lucha-Burns

Learn Thru Play: Creative Activities That Build Attention, Curiosity, and Collaboration is a collection of creative, eclectic information and activities honed from Professor Lucha-Burns's many decades of teaching and inspiring future educators. For experienced teachers and those seeking to expand their expertise in play and puppetry, this text contains hundreds of ideas to enhance the imagination and creativity in a classroom.

Trish Lindberg, PhD Professor, Plymouth State University, Coordination Integrated Arts

Learn Thru Play:

Creative Activities That Build Attention, Curiosity, and Collaboration

By Carol Lucha-Burns

Cover Design by Anniella Pettingill
Photos by Perry A. Smith and Abby Hoppe
Type setting by John M. Burns

Printed in the United States of America

Copyright and Publisher

Learn Thru Play: Creative Activities That Build Attention, Curiosity, and Collaboration

Copyright ©2024 by Lucha-Burns, LLC

All rights reserved. No part of this book may be reproduced or utilized in any form or by any means, electronic or mechanical, including photocopying, recording, or by any information storage and retrieval system, without written permission of the publisher, except by reviewers who may quote brief excerpts in connection with the review. Scanning, uploading, and distributing this book via the Internet or any other means without the publisher's permission is illegal and legally punishable.

Every effort has been made to identify copyright holders and obtain their permission for the use of copyrighted materials in this book. If you believe there has been an oversight in this regard, please be in touch directly with the author.

ISBN: 978-0-9882957-6-6

PO Box 10
Whitefield, NH 03598-
United States of America

Contents

Dedication	1
Preface	2
Introduction	5
Before Starting	8
Games	10
Games To Try	12
Art Games	12
Art Gallery	12
A Clay Play	12
Emotion Commotion	13
The Ad Fad	13
Garden Graffiti	14
I Heard it on the Grapevine	14
Illustrate and Imitate	15
Plural Murals	15
Painted History	16
Docent for a Day	16
Something's Coming	16
Statue Sculpting	17
Geography Games	18
The World Bank	18
Country for a Day	18
Frostbite	19
Twelve Question Geography	19
Archeology Digging Adventure	19
The Ending Matters	20
Map 'N Adventure	20
Know Your Capitals Spelled AL	21
Statehood Slogan or Description	21
Wonders Hall of Fame	22
Spin the Globe	22
Stamp Tales	23
What's Your Line?	23
History Games	25

Discovery	25
Art Meets History	25
Distinctive Debates	25
Significant Inventions	26
People, Places and Events	26
Life for a Week	27
What If?	27
Report the News	28
T.V. Interview	28
History Overthrown	29
Meet the Press	29
Quotation Charades	30
Scavenger Hunt	30
You're Getting Warmer	30
The Tunnel of Time	31
You Are There	31
Language Art Games	**33**
Act as an Adverb	33
Alphabet Emotion Mime	33
Alphabet Soup	34
Book Act	34
A Sherlock Holmes Mystery	34
Fun Limericks	35
Modern Myths	35
Magic Bottle Alphabet	36
We Go Together	36
Dr. Grammar	37
Newsy News	37
Proverbial Charades	37
Round Robin Slow Motion	38
Treasure Trove Titles	38
Western Union	39
What's in a Word	39
Why Onomatopoeia?	39
And the Answer is…	40
Descriptions Matter	40
Math Games	**41**
Act a Number	41
All Roads Lead to Rome	41

Food Store Frolic	42
Guilty or Not Guilty	42
A Familiar Riddle Acted	43
Metric Training	44
Math Combo	44
Number Story	45
Story Plus or Minus	45
Time Will Tell	46
A Town Takes Shape	46
Up, Up, and A Weigh	47
What's Cooking?	47
Music Games	**49**
Act the Song	49
Titles Count	49
A - One, A - Two, A - Three	49
Battle of the Biggies	50
Jug Opry	50
Zounds! Life Sounds	51
Musical Art	51
Music Culture	51
Music Of the City	52
Sounds of Nature	52
Musical Theatre	53
Musical Humor	53
Set the Mood	53
Lion Hunt Adaptation	54
Song Search	54
Tell a Tale of Music	55
This is Your Song	55
Tim—bbb —rrr	55
Science Games	**57**
Ancient Myths	57
Don't Rain on My Parade	57
Fish Gotta Swim, Birds Gotta Fly	57
Frog Cycle	58
Involvement Science	58
Keep It Moving	58
The Nature of Nature	59
Survival	59

Plant a Garden	60
Put It to Good Use	60
Scientists of the Round Table	60
Sell Your Product	61
Sideshow Science	61
Solar System	62
Voyage Through the Body	62
Weather or Not	62
Puppetry	**64**
Puppets Made Easy	**66**
Shadow and Bunraku Puppets	66
Household Object Puppets	68
Milk Carton Puppet	68
Carrot Puppet	69
Paper Bag Puppets	69
Sock Puppets	70
Marionette Style Paper Plate Puppet	72
Hand Style Paper Plate Puppet	73
Tennis Ball Style Puppet	73
Spoon Puppet	74
Fly Swatter Puppet	74
Cloth Puppet Animals	75
The Dragon Puppet	75
Costuming Clay, Paper Maché or Styrofoam	78
Production Advice	**83**
Staging Advice	**85**
Puppet Plays for Performance	**86**
Jack and The Beanstalk	86
To Philadelphia	98
Learning History In A Fun Way	**107**
Story Theatre	**108**
Paul Revere's Ride	111
Stone Stew	123
The Blind Men and The Elephant	131
Casey At The Bat	137
Involvement Theatre	**143**

Communications	146
You Were There	156
Movie In The Making	169
Finale	180
About the Author	182
About the Artist	183

Dedication

In 1969, the University of New Hampshire had only two classes in Children's Theatre. Within a few years of my arrival, there were four more. Each class required many mimeographed pages of information because no single text covered the materials included in a fifteen-week semester. Those class handouts eventually morphed into several spiral-bound texts. Over the years, various alums have urged me to develop those spiral-bound pamphlets into a series of easy-to-follow texts. *Learn Thru Play: Creative Activities That Build Attention, Curiosity, and Collaboration* is the first in the series.

Since I have always believed in Oscar Hammerstein's lyric, "…by your pupils, you'll be taught," it is time to shout out an enormous thank you to those whose knowledge and continuing assistance have been a valuable addition to this text. The following information and suggestions come from teaching undergraduates and graduates of diverse backgrounds, nationalities, ages, and majors. Thanks to their ideas and creativity, which enhanced this work, and are now preserved for readers to utilize and expand upon. I dedicate this work to all my students and our mutual creative inventiveness.

Thanks also to former colleagues Pat Gallagher, John Garand, Susan Goldin, Sarah Marschner, and Pat Northridge. A special thanks to Anniella Pettingill for the cover design and copy editing and to puppet illustrator Linda M. Lyons. A special thanks goes to my very patient, supportive, and loving spouse, John M. Burns.

Preface

By Cecilia Dintino

Assistant Clinical Professor of Psychology

The relationship between play and learning is best seen and grasped in the context of children. How do children learn? They play. They create, they imagine, and they pretend. Implementing the arts into any curriculum can enhance a child's attention, engagement, and curiosity.

What does it mean to learn? How best can one foster a learning experience?

These questions have been considered and re-considered for decades. Some educators, such as Carol Lucha-Burns, have explored answers to these questions and can provide guidelines for the rest of us who aim to teach or foster development in children.

Developmental Psychologist Alison Gopnick of the University of California, Berkeley, has done numerous studies examining how children learn best. Her findings indicate that playful exploration and interaction with materials, as well as with others, breeds creative problem-solving, discovery, and long-term retention of information. In addition, the mere act of pretending appears to promote focus, perseverance, and follow-through on tasks.

Dr. Charles Limb of Johns Hopkins University shows us how creative improvisation heightens brain activity, as demonstrated by his FMRI studies. He explains how his research on improvisation and spontaneity proves that creative impulses stimulate cognitive growth more than memorized or rote learning.

It's the art of discovery that teaches best; the process vs the product that yields the juiciest fruit.

Psychologist Carol Dweck's mindset studies depict two types of thinking, fixed and growth. A child with a fixed mindset is more concerned with looking smart and getting it right, whereas a child with a growth mindset is interested in the process, has a desire to learn, and is willing to participate in an exploration without the fear of making mistakes. Dweck suggests that a growth mindset is a "passport to new adventures," a lifetime of curiosity.

And too, the act of collaboration has a role in how children learn best. Anthropologist Lewis Dean compared a group of chimpanzees with a group of children in a puzzle-solving exercise. The children solved the puzzle faster than the chimpanzees by using one important method: they worked together. The children shared ideas and built upon the others' discoveries. The chimps worked alone.

This is a formula for learning that is vital and promising. It requires curiosity, spontaneity, and sharing. We have a method that utilizes this formula. It's called the arts, which itself relies on the techniques and practices of play.

We could all use inspiration, guidance, and a blueprint for including the arts in the learning process. Carol Lucha-Burns' book offers just this. Tried and true exercises that include art, music, puppetry, story, and drama for all subjects and all classrooms.

If we can make learning an act of play that stimulates curiosity and incorporates the whole child - body, mind, and spirit - we will have a better chance of capturing the child's attention and commitment to the process of discovery. Along with grades and standardized testing scores, each child deserves opportunities to learn in ways that involve them in enthusiastic, creative play with enthusiastic others.

This book will show you how. Enjoy.

Cecilia Dintino: Assistant Clinical Professor of Psychology Columbia University Medical Center. Adjunct Faculty of the Graduate Program in Drama Therapy at New York University.

Introduction

This handbook is based on surviving a lifetime with ADHD long before the connected letters became household words. In my public school, the elementary years were focused on developing the "whole child"; hence, the teachers did not focus on competitive grades but wrote quarterly and insightful evaluation letters on every student. My parents knew about my "wandering attention" but had no idea why. My well-educated, former Latin teacher, Mom, often looked at me in confusion and lovingly told me, "If you didn't look so much like your father's side of the family, I would think there was a mix-up in the hospital." I found it enlightening (as a tenured and award-winning, published university professor) to read my fourth-grade teacher's enthusiastic report letter that "we got Carol to sit down for an entire lunch period."

Mom's annual Christmas Letters filled in the trajectory of my very social life that was hyper-focused on helping wherever needed. I did more stage managing of others than academically managing myself. As I rediscovered those holiday letters that took me from fourth grade through obtaining the University of Utah's first MFA in Children's Theatre, I realized that much of my success was due to my living and learning through the lens of my love affair with the arts.

My teaching experience as a university Professor with ADHD who taught students with many of those same characteristics, i.e., missing assignments, being easily distracted, lacking organization, and being inattentive (the list goes on), indicated a need for the information in this publication. *Learn Thru Play: Creative Activities That*

Build Attention, Curiosity, and Collaboration gives the reader/leader/teacher/student various ideas to utilize and expand upon.

The participants will have a chance to develop through the use of games, puppetry, Story Theatre, and Involvement Plays, the following:

1. Communication skills. In the variety of games and plays, the leader and the students must communicate with other characters on stage and with the audience.

2. Self-confidence. Interactive and discussion-oriented games allow the students to gain confidence in their ideas and their ability to present themselves convincingly.

3. Creative problem-solving. The art of adaptability and the necessity of versatility. Creative decisions must be made, often during a performance in front of a live audience. After all, the show must go on. The more experiences students have, where they learn through the process of doing, of problem-solving in real-time, and through that process, discovering that they have the ability to achieve under pressure, is often more valuable than learning the correct answer in a solo situation. This aids in the "growth mindset" goal for students who desire to learn through the process rather than needing to have the "right" answer. Consistent work in this style helps increase attention and follow-through.

4. Collaboration and team-play. This book contains games and plays that aim to increase team-building skills, enhance listening and self-awareness, and further develop interactive relationships.

5. Group participation and the ensemble experience: working as a group to create something from start to finish. Respect for authority and the rules of organization. The participants must learn quickly to abide by the group's rules as the games are being played and as they create their own plays. There is a sense of individual as well as group achievement in experiencing a product from creation to completion.

6. Collaboration and ensemble commitment to the final result allows a growth process that requires trust and leads to respect for everyone in every position, no matter how small. Working as an ensemble helps increase attention and follow-through.

7. Ideally, the group will represent today's diverse world, and the collaboration of participants with different histories and backgrounds should lead the teacher and the team to discover materials that will build a tolerance for those differences and opportunities to encounter other perspectives.

This book is meant to be an inspiration as well as a guide. Everyone with a flair for play and a sense of humor will find this a valuable handbook for the classroom, library, summer camp, home-school, and after-school program. The focus is on the leader to help guide the others as they become involved in group development. The group learns by doing, watching, being physically involved, laughing, and absorbing. Interested groups should enjoy performing some of the included plays (complete with acting directions and comments) or writing their own for presentation. This text contains examples that anyone may freely use in educational settings.

Before Starting

For the leader, an essential piece of information to remember is to believe in your ability to succeed. Almost anything is possible with your group if they believe that you think that what you're doing is the best, most exciting, and most "fun" thing imaginable. And believe me, it is fun. The more you venture into this work and experiment with the variety of exercises within, the more your trust in yourself will expand

Never panic!!! This method is usually one of trial and error. Some days and with some groups, anything will work; others exist to test your resourceful abilities. Always admit that something needs "tweaking" and that "we" might want to try something different. Only stop something after giving it a chance to succeed or fail. Always feel free to discuss any problem areas with the group. Ask for their suggestions and thus incorporate the entire situation into a team learning effort. The more the group as a whole is involved in their learning process, the easier and more productive the process.

The leader will want to set ground rules that the group understands. The most successful explanation is that "a successful activity depends upon mutual respect." Thus, a possible problem, such as noise, is alleviated by the teams' realization that too much talking and commotion will interfere with their ability to hear each other and, therefore, prevent them from fulfilling their goal.

Always remember that this is something you like doing. Your sense of enjoyment and excitement will be contagious. The basic premise of *Learn Thru Play: Creative Activities That Build Attention, Curiosity, and*

Collaboration is that "we" have something worth developing together. Using the arts, games, and plays to help your students discover, learn, and, most importantly, retain material is a proven way of "spicing" up the learning process.

Games

The first part of the book includes one hundred-seven games that may be adapted for various age levels. These self-explanatory games are divided into the following categories: Art, Geography, History, Language Arts, Math, Music, and Science. Certain games that have been written for a particular subject can easily be adapted to other topics. These are only introductory approaches to stimulate your imagination to create others.

Some activities may require prepared materials, such as world maps, examples of famous art, an instrumental piece of music, etc. The students will need to be able to access these materials before and during the sessions where they are needed. Most may be found in a library or on the Internet.

In many of these activities, arbitrary numbers of participants are used to demonstrate how to "play" the game. Most games may be done in smaller units, with a few individuals, or even with a larger group. It may be helpful to start off with a few games that intrigue you and that you feel can be successful in your situation. The more you gauge the group response, the more you will discover about the success of the exercise and how a response may be improved by altering sections of the game.

Please remember that these games are only an impetus designed to bring collaboration in various ways. The rest is up to the teacher/leader. The assignment to the university undergraduate and graduate level students in my Education Through Dramatization course was to submit a series of subject-based games using the following categories: Art, Geography, History, Language Arts, Math, Music, and

Science for grades three and up. They created games appropriate to the ages they planned on teaching. As the games were presented and tested in the college classroom, the group discovered that the games were well-suited to be adapted to a different topic or age range. The leader with experience will know if a game suits their specific class and teaching goals. Those with limited practical knowledge of various school ages are encouraged to jump in and freely adjust any exercises to meet their needs. These games are included to stimulate your imagination and inspire you. Adjust and change them as you need.

Games To Try

Art Games

Art Gallery

Procedure: Each participant chooses a famous painter, researches their work, collects prints (from the library or Internet) of the artist's works, and joins with other "artists" of the period or style to create a "gallery" of work. The group is then responsible for displaying the prints in the classroom and inviting other students to view their "gallery." The students may question the artist's style and technique. Additionally, individual artists may direct audience/classroom members to re-create each famous painting. This re-enactment helps the viewers remember the picture.

Note: These may be set up by artistic movement (Renaissance), country (Italy), or style (Abstract). This game is not limited to an art class. It may also be utilized effectively in a history and social studies class.

A Clay Play

Procedure: Each student makes a clay figure of a specific character. The facial expression must be clearly shown, and the posture or position is essential to the character. After the clay models harden, the class divides into small groups. Each student (with eyes closed) in each group then touches a clay model (not their own) and develops a character based on their interpretation of the clay model. Each student then acts out this character for the group, and the group improvises a play involving all the characters.

Note: This game develops sensory awareness and forces participants to focus on the specifics of a given character. It works best for a small group. Some teachers have utilized the descriptions in Dickens' books as inspiration.

Emotion Commotion

Procedure: The teacher plays music while the participants paint a design with materials suited to their age group, i.e., finger painting for the younger ones. The art is an interpretation of what they hear. After discussing the various emotions the music evokes, they may team up with others to create a group play or choose to enact their feelings based on their art as the music is replayed.

Note: This game can combine drama, music, art, and dance.

The Ad Fad

Procedure: The class is divided into small groups, and each group creates a book based on visual advertisements from print or online sources. They then create a title and improvise a play based on one or more of the visuals. The wilder the characters, the more fun. The plays should be about ten minutes long.

Note: Windex. We saw right through it.

Mr. Clean came to the rescue.

Garden Graffiti

Procedure: Individually, each group member draws a picture of something with a unique name in a garden. They must characterize the object of the drawing. The class divides into groups of four and decides on a scene using various plant characteristics.

Note: Poison Ivy;
Snap Dragon;
Venus Fly Trap;
Impatiens.

I Heard it on the Grapevine

Procedure: Students draw their favorite fruit or vegetable and give their object facial expressions and body features. They then act out the character of their fruit or vegetable when it becomes something else. In order to save time, the student may draw the picture at home but act it out for the class before showing the art.

Note: Grape Turning Into a Raisin;
Cucumber Into a Pickle;
Sour-Faced Lemon Being Squeezed.

Illustrate and Imitate

Procedure: Everyone must illustrate an incident in a story or poem, emphasizing individual character types. Subsequently, the characters come to life (individually or in a group) when the acting begins. This game allows the student to develop characters. In *A Christmas Carol*, the party scene at the nephew's house allows the artist to develop visual-spatial and character relationships as well as draw the various characters in period costumes. Individual class members may begin a scene "in the art" and act a portion of the story.

Note: Age-dependent: Nursery Rhymes, Fairy Tales, Folk Tales, Poetry, or Dickens' descriptions.

Plural Murals

Procedure: The team decides on a country to depict on their mural and chooses representative objects. Each artist is allowed space on the mural/s. These murals may exemplify a study of a location, familiar landmarks, or what the area is best known for. The completed mural may become the backdrop for an improvisation. This may also be included in a section on history by adding a specific situation.

Note: Japan: Rice Fields, Kimonos, Temples, Mt. Fuji, Buddha;

London: Royal Guard, Buckingham Palace, Tower Bridge, Big Ben;

Paris: The Eiffel Tower, Notre Dame, The Louvre.

Painted History

Procedure: Using famous portraits by well-known artists, individuals research what it was like to live in that period, create a situation, and act it out with specific individuals portraying the person(s) in the picture.

Note: American Gothic, Paul Revere's Ride, George Washington Crossing the Delaware.

Docent for a Day

Procedure: Each student creates a situational painting with details such as location, character, and clothing appropriate to the era, as well as facial expressions that clarify the action. They may then serve as a museum docent/curator and take the rest of the class on an imaginary walk through the picture. It is essential to include the artist's concept for the painting.

Note: This exercise may be done in pairs, individually, or as a small group. It is also perfect for a combined art and history project.

Something's Coming

Procedure: In small groups: The group creates sets and backdrops from string or yarn. After the setting is created, people pair up to create a dramatic situation that may occur in the scene. This is a good activity for the end of winter when the days are overcast as it may focus on the coming of a new season and, depending on the level, be a simple style of art. Suitable for younger artists.

Note: A Crocus Forcing Its Way Through the Snow; A Shivering Robin Who Arrived Too Soon; A Disgruntled Snowman Melting Slowly.

Statue Sculpting

Procedure: One person acts as a sculptor. Using a unit of approximately seven to nine people as a block of material, the sculptor molds that block. Height, shape, and three-dimensional perspective (using all four sides) are utilized. To do this, the sculptor must verbally move, mold, and shape the "material" (other group members) into the relationship and shape they want.

Note: This exercise is designed to develop a simple awareness of the principles of sculpture and requires the sculptor to convey through specifics the images for others to achieve.

Learn Thru Play

Geography Games

The World Bank

Procedure: Groups of three or four study the tradable commodities and currency exchange values for a country. They then create believable characters from their countries and negotiate trade with each other. Each group establishes a dramatic situation to enact.

Note: This exercise encourages the research of culture, attributes, commodities, currency, and situations that may be affected by geography. Through acting, the students show an understanding of the above. It may also be a math exercise as it deals with currency exchange.

Country for a Day

Procedure: Depending on how long you want the project to take, use the entire class or divide it into smaller groups. Collect or make various objects that reflect the culture of a specific country. Organize a space (or spaces) for various countries. The entire group, or in smaller units, then improvise a play to reflect the country's lifestyle and culture.

Note: Japan - Cultivating Rice Fields, Earthquakes;

France - Wine-Making, Cooking;

Mexico - Piñata Party, Weaving, Jewelry.

Learn Thru Play

Frostbite

Procedure: An outside activity might be the re - creation of an Eskimo village with the group enacting village life (i.e., building igloos, catching fish, etc).

Note: Outside activities can stimulate interest because they extend the physical boundaries of one's location.

Twelve Question Geography

Procedure: Individuals choose a geographical term or definition to act out while others guess the word. This may be done as a review before a test or to introduce new material.

Note: Peninsula, a landform surrounded (for the most part) by water;

Glacier, a field or body of ice moving by its own weight;

Strait, a comparatively narrow passageway connecting two large bodies of water.

Archeology Digging Adventure

Procedure: Divide into fours and choose a location for an archeological dig. Assemble pictures, crafts, or drawings chronicling the objects found in the dig. A day in the life of "their people" may follow.

Note: This allows the students to develop an

understanding of how modern civilizations were founded.

The Ending Matters

Procedure: One person acts out something specific about a country while the others guess the activity and the country. The individual who guesses correctly must act out something for another nation whose name begins with the last letter of the land previously guessed.

Note: Act out The Sphinx - Egypt; (T is the new letter)

Act out Thai Dancers - Thailand begins with the letter T, the last letter of Egypt;

Act out The Little Mermaid - Thailand's final letter is D - hence Denmark;

Act out cultivating or eating rice - K - Korea.

Map 'N Adventure

Procedure: The group is divided into threes, and someone chooses a location from a hat. Each group is responsible for charting the shortest route from a given point to its location. Upon completing their map, they act out the journey from start to finish (for younger groups, a portion of their journey); others guess where they went.

Note: This exercise may vary according to age level and the country being studied. It may also include mathematical measurements.

Learn Thru Play

Know Your Capitals Spelled AL

Procedure: The group draws an outline map of the United States on paper and places it on a wall or an area of open floor. The group is divided into two teams, A and B. The leader calls out the name of a State. Member one from team A has the first chance to run to the capital of that state, name it, and act out a major industry. Another state is called out, and a member from team B has the first chance to run to that state's capital. If member one of team B doesn't know the answer, then member two of team A has a turn.

Note: This game may be expanded to include cities, products, and industries. If desired, it may also include historical data and geographical topography. This is also a good outside activity with chalk-drawn maps.

Statehood Slogan or Description

Procedure: Individuals act out a State name, description, or nickname for others to guess.

Note: Smallest State - Rhode Island;
Sunshine State - Florida;
Granite State - New Hampshire;
Garden State - New Jersey.

Learn Thru Play

Wonders Hall of Fame

Procedure: Divide into groups of four and have each group determine three modern Wonders of the World. One group must then act out their wonder for the rest of the class to guess. After the Wonders are all guessed, everyone votes to see what, if anything, should be added to the Wonders Hall of Fame. The teacher may assign each group a different continent.

Note: The Statue of Liberty;
The Tokyo Tower;
Mount Rushmore;
The Panama Canal;
The Chesapeake Bay Bridge.

Spin the Globe

Procedure: One blindfolded team member stands before a globe while another spins the globe. The blindfolded person puts a finger on the globe, and wherever it is touched becomes the team's Country of the Week. Various aspects of the Country will be studied and subsequently acted on. If the area pointed to is an Ocean, an Island or nearby Country is chosen.

Note: This gives familiarity with the globe and is a spontaneous way to choose an area of study. The game may be expanded to include several Countries. Find a common thread that links them and proceed with the above exercise. If several of the chosen areas were once part of a

European Nation, Colonization may be an interesting topic.

Stamp Tales

Procedure: Everyone brings in stamps from various geographical locations. These may be found online. Stamps that depict a story rather than just a picture of a famous person are a better choice. Divide into small groups by region, i.e., those who pick stamps from Africa can be in one group and Latin America another. Each group chooses a stamp and works together to create a playlet using the stamp as a catalyst.

Note: International stamps may show how each country projects its national image. By focusing on a region, similarities may be discovered.

What's Your Line?

Procedure: A hat is filled with words denoting various occupations. Someone takes a card and acts out the selected employment particular to a specific region or country. Upon completion of the activity, everyone guesses the occupation and country. The person with the correct answer chooses the next profession card. As many careers are utilized in various geographical locations, the group must be able to demonstrate their knowledge through specific acting choices.

Note: This game demonstrates the various occupations that a country may be noted for. This exercise requires some background information and an active imagination.

Cowboy - American West or Argentina;

Bullfighter - Spain or South America;

Camel Driver - Egypt or The Middle East;

Goat, Cow, or Sheep Herder - Switzerland.

Learn Thru Play

History Games

Discovery

Procedure: The leader writes a list of clues on slips of paper and hides them around the room. The discovery of each new clue is dependent upon the previous one. Participants are divided into small exploring parties and become different famous explorers and their crews. They will search out and use only those clues that apply to their explorer's discovery.

Note: Ponce DeLeon - Florida;

Magellan - The World Is Round;

Balboa - The Pacific Ocean;

De Soto - The Mississippi River.

Art Meets History

Procedure: Divide into small groups and portray a famous painted or sculpted historical moment. The group portraying the "moment" should be able to explain the history behind the art.

Note: Washington Crossing the Delaware;

Raising the Flag on Iwo Jima;

Paul Revere's Ride.

Distinctive Debates

Procedure: Divide the larger group into pairs. Each pair decides upon their historical figures, creates their own unique debate topic, and dramatically improvises the situation. This requires background knowledge of historical characters. The historical figures should be from different eras and locations and have very different points of view. See below for suggestions.

Note: Henry VIII vs. Gloria Steinem;

Thomas Jefferson vs. George III;

Beethoven vs. Elton John.

Significant Inventions

Procedure: The leader serves as Dr. History and calls on individuals to portray an inventor (whose background has been researched). After the "inventor" has explained their invention and its significance to Dr. History, the inventor and Dr. History physically create the invention using others if needed. The "inventor" must be knowledgeable about their invention and be able to answer questions that demonstrate an understanding of the period and the impact of the discovery.

Note: Eli Whitney - The Cotton Gin;

Robert Fulton - The Steamboat;

Elias Howe - The Sewing Machine.

People, Places and Events

Procedure: The leader chooses a historic event requiring group participation. Individuals may either volunteer or be assigned roles. Research is required to develop characters for the individuals being portrayed. The sophistication and age level of the group will determine attention to detail and exact interpretation of the period.

Note: Building the Panama Canal;

Building the Transcontinental Railroad;

Laying the Trans-Atlantic Cable.

Life for a Week

Procedure: The classroom becomes a specific historical setting for one week. During that time, the students become citizens and participants in that setting. Activities may include daily, economic, cultural, sporting, and political activities (those things that would make up life in ??? during the period of ???. This is important because the students maintain a consistent character throughout the entire week.

Note: Life in a Colonial Town;

Life in a Medieval Castle;

Life in a Japanese Village;

Life in Ancient Greece.

What If?

Procedure: Speeches and various moments in history may be used. The skits may be historical events that never took place or actual events from the past.

It will require a thorough knowledge of the principal players of the times for speeches to be created and scenes to be acted. This would be for older students involved in a longer classroom activity.

Note: If Burr Hadn't Killed Alexander Hamilton;

If Benjamin Franklin Had Run for President;

If Lincoln Hadn't Been Shot.

Report the News

Procedure: In small groups, develop a half-hour newscast based on a specific historical period. Individuals are responsible for a particular news story based on a historical fact, supplemented by additional human interest stories that reflect the period.

Note: Take a Typical Day in History, i.e., July 1, 1776. General News Reports on a Continuing Meeting of the Continental Congress. These may include;

Caesar Rodney at home in Delaware;

Reports from the Front Lines - Yorktown;

Economic Report, i.e., Shipping and Cotton;

Daily Quote from Poor Richard's Almanac.

T.V. Interview

Procedure: One person serves as an interviewer, while another portrays a historical figure. Character development, knowledge of the times, and culture will require thorough research.

Note: Thomas Paine on the writing of Common Sense;

George Washington Carver on crop diversity;

John Ringling on a three-ring Circus.

History Overthrown

Procedure: A historical scene or event is chosen and initiated. After the situation is established, individuals may call out a change. Players must incorporate the change while remaining consistent with their characters. Actors must try and get back to the "real history."

Note: The Mayflower decides to turn back;

Marie Antoinette's Guillotine sticks;

Henry VIII doesn't divorce his first wife.

Meet the Press

Procedure: Individuals are responsible for portraying famous person(s) during a historic event. They make a press statement explaining the situation while the remainder of the group serves as the press corps and asks questions.

Note: Thomas Jefferson on the writing of the Declaration of Independence;

Abraham Lincoln on the slavery issue;

Harry Truman on the recalling of General MacArthur.

Quotation Charades

Procedure: There are two teams (A and B). Each team writes famous quotations (one per slip of paper) for the opposition team to enact. The first-team member draws a slip of paper and must act out the quote for the team. Then, the other team takes a turn.

Note: "Give Me Liberty or Give Me Death;"

"I Have Not Yet Begun To Fight;"

"The Only Thing We Have To Fear Is Fear Itself."

Scavenger Hunt

Procedure: Divide into groups of four. Each group makes up a scavenger list for a given group of people at a specific time. They then act out their list, and the others guess individual items and the overall scene the team is trying to portray.

Note: San Antonio at the time of the Alamo;

Tokyo at the time of the 1923 Earthquake;

Opening of the Eiffel Tower, Paris, France.

You're Getting Warmer

Procedure: Small groups decide on a moment of history they wish to depict. They then freeze in a position that depicts the "moment in history" while the other members guess. Guesses close to the correct answer thaw the statue, and the group slowly begins physical operation. A wrong guess will re-freeze them.

Note: Pilgrims landing on Plymouth Rock;

Lincoln at Ford's Theatre;

Carving Mt. Rushmore.

The Tunnel of Time

Procedure: The group divides into smaller units to decide what moment of history they wish to portray. The entire class creatively builds (through physical movement) a time machine capable of transporting a small unit back in time. The unit transported back must portray the time or event of their choice and can only return to the present when the people in the present correctly guess the period and situation.

Note: Boston - 1773;

Chicago - 1871;

New York - 1929

You Are There

Procedure: Students divide into groups of five and choose a historical event (possibly related to the unit material being studied). They have the option of improvising or scripting their chosen historical moment.

Note: The Pony Express;

The first Telephone Message;

Invention of the Motion Picture.

Language Art Games

Act as an Adverb

Procedure: Small groups are established. One member of each group leaves the room while the remaining members decide on an adverb. When the person returns, different group members are asked to perform an activity (e.g., eating), which they must enact using the quality of the adverb.

Note: Cry - slowly;

Eat - quickly;

Laugh - happily.

Alphabet Emotion Mime

Procedure: The first volunteer pantomimes an emotion beginning with the letter A; the second volunteer pantomimes a feeling with the letter B, etc. When no emotion for a letter can be thought of, the game jumps to another letter. The class must guess the feeling. Suitable for younger students.

Note: A - Angry;

B - Blue;

C - Carefree;

D - Depressed;

E - Elated.

Alphabet Soup

Procedure: The group is given a noun, and the participants must pantomime that noun, adding adjectives that start with a specific letter.

Note: Elephant is the Noun, and C is the letter;

Crazy Elephant;

Cute Elephant;

Clumsy Elephant.

Book Act

Procedure: After reading or discussing a story, individuals or a group of participants act out an important event in the book. The leader may choose a specific section that utilizes a topic for discussion.

Note: *Charlotte's Web* - Templeton's "crunchy" find;

The Wizard of Oz - The Wicked Witch melting;

A Christmas Carol - The Spirits visit Scrooge.

A Sherlock Holmes Mystery

Procedure: The teacher guides the entire class through the creation of an Involvement story based on parts of speech. This is the perfect exercise for older students to perform for younger grades.

Note: *The Case of the Lost Verbs;*

The Case of the Missing Pronouns;

The Case of the Dangling Participle.

Fun Limericks

Procedure: This exercise follows a discussion and explanation of limericks. This may be done in a group or individually. A short scene is played for the group. Those watching create limericks about the enactment. This may also be done in reverse, with a student writing a limerick and having a group enact it.

Note: This exercise allows working with the rhythm and rhyming of words and is a fun introduction to poetry, i.e.;
There was an odd fellow named Gus,
When traveling, he made such a fuss.
He was banned from the train,
Not allowed on a plane,
And now travels only by bus.

Modern Myths

Procedure: The students write new and updated versions of the ancient myths and act them out for the class.

Note: This exercise gives the students a background in myths and legends while allowing for various interpretations and adaptations. Pandora's Box is a myth about evils released to the world. Modern versions of her story could concern current diseases, i.e., the flu.

Learn Thru Play

Magic Bottle Alphabet

Procedure: The teacher tells a story about a magic bottle that contains different objects. The students are to take an object from the bottle and depict it in pantomime. Each student's object should begin with progressive alphabet letters. At first glance, this exercise appears very basic for older students, but it can be modified to teach a new language or unfamiliar science vocabulary,

Note: D - Devil;

E - Elephant;

F - Frankfurt;

G - Goldfish;

H - Hyena.

We Go Together

Procedure: Two groups are established. One group has one set of words, while the other holds pairing words. While individuals in the first group pantomime its terms, individuals in the second group seek and find their partner. After everyone is matched, each pair pantomimes their paired action for the class. (The couples may not ask questions or tell what they are).

Note: Pal Words - Bow and Arrow; Rod and Reel; Nouns and Verbs - Fish Swim, Birds Fly; Opposites - Up and Down; Hot, and Cold.

Learn Thru Play

Dr. Grammar

Procedure: Everyone portrays a part of speech and must be prepared to enact and (when asked) explain why their part of speech is essential. The speech and physical characterization should reflect the particular part of speech represented. This game assists students in remembering the purpose of the various parts of speech and the roles they play.

Note: Noun - Very Subjective;

Adverb - A Dependent Character;

Verb - Action-oriented.

Newsy News

Procedure: Students divide into groups and decide on a famous bit of news to enact. The rest of the class must write news stories using a specific number of words and column inches. It may be more focused if there is a school newspaper that students submit articles to.

Note: This would be more meaningful if a trip to an actual newspaper office preceded or followed.

Proverbial Charades

Procedure: Students act out (individually or in pairs) proverbs or sayings. Short skits may be improvised based on the adage.

Note: A stitch in time saves nine;

A fool and his money are soon parted;

Early to bed and early to rise.

Round Robin Slow Motion

Procedure: One person volunteers to start a story while the rest of the group moves slowly within the room's space. The person must keep the story going until they tag the first "character." The person tagged assumes the character's role in the previous part of the story and continues by adding a new character for the next person.

Note: This game encourages character development and focus. The participants must pay attention to four things at once: avoiding being tagged, listening, continuing the story, and portraying a character.

Treasure Trove Titles

Procedure: The teacher hides slips of paper with vocabulary words representing different parts of speech. The class is divided into groups, and based on the words discovered, they must create a title for an improvised short skit. They may rehearse and perform the improvised play for another class or just for each other.

Note: The value of this exercise lies in demonstrating knowledge of the parts of speech used in a correct sentence and developing a play around a single sentence.

Western Union

Procedure: A group of students acts out a situation while the rest of the class must compose an appropriate ten-word telegram.

Note: This game forces the student to be observant and concise. It is good for students working on a school newspaper.

What's in a Word

Procedure: The teacher lists new vocabulary words on the board. Students divide into groups of three. Each group must find the definition of its word and devise a skit to show it and its meaning to the rest of the class. Acting the word in a given situation may help the participants retain the exact meaning of the word. Picking similar words makes this more difficult.

Note: Sinister,

Boisterous,

Flamboyant.

Why Onomatopoeia?

Procedure: The class makes up a list of words that sound the same as their action; they then divide into small groups and act out the words. They may create a play around several of the words. This is an age-dependent exercise.

Note: Choo Choo Train;

Cackling Geese;

Babbling Brook.

And the Answer is…

Procedure: For a book test review, the teacher creates slips of paper with the author's name and the title of a book by that author. Each class member draws a slip of paper from a container, which they proceed to act out. The class guesses the book title and author. This is very much like the popular parlor game of charades.

Note: Frank Baum - *The Wizard of Oz;*

Dr. Seuss - *Horton Hatches the Egg;*

Maurice Sendak - *Where the Wild Things Are.*

Descriptions Matter

Procedure: Individual members of the group choose a character they wish to portray to those in the audience. This may be mimed or with ad-libbed words. After each individual's "character" has finished, the participants write a five-minute story about the character, focusing on facial expressions, movement style, habits, etc., and location.

Note: Allowing participants to see a character acted out in a specific environment often entices them to write more detailed descriptive passages.

Learn Thru Play

Math Games

Act a Number

Procedure: Each student chooses a number to represent to the group. By his actions, the group can tell what type of character or situation is being portrayed and what number it is. This game may be mimed or with dialogue. To make the game more understandable, the numbers being enacted should be limited and written on the whiteboard.

Note: 1 - Straight Forward - British Man;

8 - Round and Friendly - Santa Claus;

5 - Level Headed - A village of people walking around with books on their heads.

All Roads Lead to Rome

Procedure: The class is divided into six groups, each representing a period in history. Using Roman Numerals, each member of the audience jots down the year the event took place. They act out the event, and the other groups must guess the moment in history.

Note: Stock Market Crash - 1929, - MCMXXIX;

Magna Carta - 1215, - MCCXV;

American Independence - 1776, - MDCCLXXVI

Learn Thru Play

Food Store Frolic

Procedure: Set up the classroom like a food store (combining this with an art project would be ideal). Have the students develop various characters as shoppers, and give each student ten dollars in scrip to spend. The one who gets the most items with the best well-balanced variety and is the closest to ten dollars without going over wins the game. One student acts as a cashier and is replaced if a mathematical error occurs.

Note: This exercise is practical and may be turned into an art project. For example, the students could bring in used tin cans and boxes to create a set for their store.

Guilty or Not Guilty

Procedure: Students volunteer to take the parts of the defendant, two lawyers, and a judge. The remaining students comprise the jury. Each lawyer asks mathematical questions, with one lawyer having the opportunity to object while the judge rules on the objection. The jurors keep track of the right and wrong answers (based on their knowledge) to determine the defendant's mathematical rating. After the lawyers present their summary, each juror will verbally rate the defendant.

Note: Judge: What is a triangle of two equal sides called?
Lawyer for Defense: "Objection."

Judge: "On what grounds?"
Lawyer for Defense: "Too difficult."
Judge: "Overruled. The defendant will answer the question."
Defendant: "Pythagorean Triangle."
At this point, the jury will mark correct or incorrect and include the right answer on their trial sheets. (Isosceles).

A Familiar Riddle Acted

Procedure: The students act out the following math riddle. A farmer is going on a long journey; he comes to a deep river and wants to get a cow, chicken, and hay on the other side of the river. There is a boat, but it can only take one thing at a time. There is a fox on the other side of the river; if the farmer puts the chicken on the same side of the river alone with the fox, the fox will eat it; if the cow and the hay are left alone together on one side of the river, the cow will eat all the hay at once and will have nothing more to eat for the rest of the journey. How can the farmer get the cow, chicken, and hay on the other side of the river?

Solution: Take the cow across; bring the fox back; take the chicken across; come back alone and get the hay across.

Note: Have five students act this out. The remainder of the class, individually or in groups, may create their own math riddle, which may be enacted. This exercise is beneficial for students who are not fond of mathematics. It gives them a chance to perform for an audience and gain respect for riddles that can be solved.

Metric Training

Procedure: The class is divided into two groups of ten each. Two members from each group volunteer to be the engineer/engine and caboose. The rest of the group will be assigned specific-length "cars" (use cardboard written numbers). The teacher, as conductor, guides the "cars" as they try to assemble a train one mile long using their displayed car lengths. Once the train is assembled, the students can become characters on a western-bound train. If one group lacks the required length, they may borrow or exchange with the other group.

Note: The teacher/conductor assigns car lengths in metric and/or USCS (customary units) units, i.e., centimeters, millimeters, inches, feet, and yards. The students must be able to figure out the conversion between English units and metric ones. To simplify the above for younger students, just add and subtract in one system.

Math Combo

Procedure: The class divides into groups of twos and carries on a conversation using only numbers to express ideas and thoughts. If the first (Individual A) comes up with the expression 3,

6, 9, the partner (Individual B) must respond with the same multiples 12, 15, 18.

Note: Individual A 4, 8, 12;

Individual B 16, 20, 24;

This exercise was a popular one in acting schools as it forced students to work on vocal variety and show dramatic emotions vocally. Of course, acting classes did not utilize the math feature of the exercise.

Number Story

Procedure: Divide into groups of four to create and act out a story using numbers and their combinations.

Note: One, who was very lonely, and zero, who felt he was just a big nothing, met one day, and they combined to form ten. They became helpful, when followed by cents, to the two children who wanted to buy some candy.

Story Plus or Minus

Procedure: The teacher tells a story involving many people or animals. The numbers rarely remain consistent, causing the students to add and subtract while staying in character throughout. The storyteller may rotate from the teacher to various students.

Note: Six children go on a walk in the woods. They come upon a grove of ten pine trees. Three woodsmen come along and chop down three trees apiece. How many people and trees are left? Then, four squirrels join the children, etc.

Time Will Tell

Procedure: A large cardboard clock is placed in the front of the room. Students volunteer to point the clock's hands to a specific time of day and pantomime or act out a two-minute skit of what usually happens at that time.

Note: 8:00 a.m. Alarm Rings, A lazy student shuts off the alarm and gets out of bed;
9:00 a.m. A harried person arrives late to work;
3:30 p.m. Exhausted Teacher says goodbye to students at the end of class;
5:30 p.m. Sarcastic Taxi Driver in rush hour traffic.

A Town Takes Shape

Procedure: The teacher creates stories about various shapes and forms while the students act them out.

Note: Once, there was a community called Circle City where everyone was round and pleasant. Squaresville was on the other side of the mountain, where everyone was very blocky and square. On the top of the mountain was the town of Triangle. (Ad-lib story of how the towns get together. Students must act out their town's shapes and any interaction between the towns).This is a good "wind down" game for the end of the day and for younger students.

Up, Up, and A Weigh

Procedure: The teacher writes various weights of cargo and baggage on individual pieces of paper and places them in a container. The class is divided into two groups: One acts as airline personnel (baggage clerk, ticket takers, etc.). Another group acts as the baggage handlers. The teacher holds a sheet of paper showing the maximum plane weight allowance for the combination of luggage and cargo. Each student draws a piece of paper from the container that states the weights of the bags and the cargo. The weights listed will be more than the allowable tonnage on the plane. The airline personnel must decide on what things are unnecessary and who and what should be left behind. Students must take on definite characters and use math logic in their arguments. To facilitate the exercise for older students, the teacher will distribute papers to each of the waiting passengers, giving them a character and ideas for why their baggage must be included. The students develop a play around the various stories.

Note: A Doctor with medicine for a sick tribe;

A Lion Tamer on the way to a Circus;

A Woodcarver with a lifetime supply of carvings.

What's Cooking?

Procedure: The teacher dons a baker's hat while the students become various fractions of ingredients according to the chosen recipe. As the baker calls for the ingredients, the students combine to form the recipe and then the final baked products. Each student has drawn a specific amount from papers in a hat, i.e. ½ cup.

Note: This exercise should be combined with a lesson on measurement equivalencies and fractions.

Bread:

1 cup of water (2 Students as ¼ Cup each and 1 student is ½ Cup). The total equals 1 cup.

Combine with 1 Package of yeast until it bubbles.

Add 1 Tablespoon of sugar (or 3 Teaspoons),

2 cups of flour (¼ cup, ½ cup, and 2 Tablespoons, 6 teaspoons, and 1 Cup). etc.

The children act out the mixture as the teacher narrates.

Music Games

Act the Song

Procedure: There are numerous songs and nursery rhymes that lend themselves to dramatization. Either divide into small groups or operate as an entire class, depending on the scope of the chosen rhymes or songs. This is an excellent introduction to drama for younger students. Older students may enjoy working with younger students to create various song-skits with movement and characters.

Note: The Farmer in the Dell;

Mary Had a Little Lamb;

This Old Man.

Titles Count

Procedure: The class is divided into small groups, and each group is responsible for miming the title of a song or a few familiar lyrics; the audience guesses when the acting is completed.

Note: I'm Looking Over a Four Leaf Clover;

If You're Happy and You Know It.

A - One, A - Two, A - Three

Procedure: The students study different types of instruments (and their families). One student becomes the conductor while the rest pantomime using other musical instruments. As each student has the opportunity to play a solo, the conductor has one chance to guess the instrument and its family. The musician then becomes the conductor.

Note: This exercise may be further enhanced if music is played in the background.

Battle of the Biggies

Procedure: The class is divided in half, half into classical and half into modern; each group decides on four composers they wish to research and represent. Individual members of the group explore the four composers and compile information. Four representatives from each group are chosen to "battle" for first place.

Note: Another class should judge the first-place winner.

Jug Opry

Procedure: Each class member is responsible for making a musical instrument for the class jug band. They then put on their own Grand Ole Opry TV show.

Note: Washboard;
Washtub Bass;
Bottle Horn;
Kazoo;
Spoons.

Learn Thru Play

Zounds! Life Sounds

Procedure: Students bring to class an object which can be used to make a sound effect. Each student, in turn, makes their sound effect while the other students interpret it through movement.

Note: This exercise may be incorporated with a music listening study to understand how everyday sounds can inspire composers, i.e., The Syncopated Clock, Flight of the Bumblebee, etc.

Musical Art

Procedure: Divide into small groups, each choosing a painting to act out to music. Each group searches for music that expresses the mood and character of the art. They then play the music and act out the mood of the painting to see if the remainder of the group knows which artwork they are presenting.

Note: Ocean Scene - Yellow Submarine;

Western Painting - Grand Canyon Suite;

William Tell Shooting an Arrow - William Tell Overture.

Music Culture

Procedure: The class studies a region of America, focusing on a specific culture of American life, and sets up a community representative of that area or culture. The students then depict life in that region or culture through a music/story combination.

Note: Ozarks - Jug Band;

Western United States - Cowboy Music;

Southwest - Mexican Guitar.

Music Of the City

Procedure: Students listen to urban sounds and act out the type of people or machines that make these sounds. They then improvise a musical skit (i.e., City Music).

Note: Jackhammer Operator;

Bus Driver;

Traffic Cop.

Sounds of Nature

Procedure: The class goes for a nature walk and concentrates on various sounds around them. At the end of the walk, each student acts out the sounds and the objects that caused these sounds. After each child has acted out three sounds, the class should recreate their walk through the combination of sounds.

Note: Chirping Bird;

Hooting Owl;

Cracking Twig.

Musical Theatre

Procedure: The class divides into small groups, each selecting a folk or fairy tale to enact. Each group writes simple songs and integrates them into the story using the basic rules of Musical Theatre production. Advanced students may create an entire play.

Note: This exercise allows the students to see the integration of story and music and how song adds depth and understanding to characters.

Musical Humor

Procedure: Members of the group decide on something musical they wish to present (tap dance, song, juggling, yodeling, pig calling, jump roping, etc.). A list is compiled, and the class writes a script incorporating everything into a funny musical production.

Note: This exercise allows everyone to participate in the creative process. Each talent must be used for the final product to succeed.

Set the Mood

Procedure: The class is divided into groups of four. Students create stories and the musical moods they wish to portray. One student is responsible for providing the spirit the group hopes to convey using various instruments (recorder, drum, tambourine, cymbal, triangle, etc.) while the others enact the story.

Note: People in the play should rotate so that all involved can show their musical talents.

Lion Hunt Adaptation

Procedure: Divide students into groups of five. Teach each group to make a specific sound, i.e., swish (rubbing palms together), clap, finger pop, etc. After each group learns a sound, the teacher narrates a story enhanced by sound effects.

Note: The above exercise uses only basic sounds that the human body can make. It is fun for students younger than the fourth grade.

Song Search

Procedure: Each student chooses a character to study and portray. They are then responsible for finding songs representing the character's personality, moods, and occupation. Characters are then presented to the class.

Note: Children uncomfortable with singing should choose a character whose emphasis is not on fine-tonal quality. The leader may also pair the students together to help each other.

Cowboy - I'm an Old Cowhand, Pecos Bill;

Farmer - The Farmer in the Dell;

Railroad - I've Been Working on the Railroad.

Tell a Tale of Music

Procedure: The class is divided into small groups. They listen to a selection of music and individually jot down dramatization ideas. The individual groups discuss their ideas and decide upon a story background to enact. The music plays twice more while each group rehearses its story.

Note: This exercise allows the students to interpret creatively while demonstrating that variety and flexibility are possible. The music enhances their thought process.

This is Your Song

Procedure: The class becomes acquainted with the music of a classical composer. The students pair up to write lyrics for one piece of the composer's music. It is helpful if the class has a synopsis of the play idea. This is similar to Walt Disney's *Sleeping Beauty*.

Note: This approach allows students to incorporate their lyrics into a famous composer's work.

Tim—bbb—rrr

Procedure: The class is divided into groups of two. Each pair of students chooses an everyday object that moves, i.e., a bouncing ball, slinky, or rocking horse. As one student enacts the object's movement, the partner controls the movement's

Learn Thru Play

speed and tempo by imitating the object's sound.

Note: This exercise teaches tempo and timbre and is also an excellent listening and following direction game.

Learn Thru Play

Science Games

Ancient Myths

Procedure: Each student researches ancient Greek and Roman myths that initially existed to explain natural phenomena. The class is divided into groups, and each story is acted out.

Note: This exercise allows the students to research ancient history and early science while working collaboratively to create and collaboratively enact their own short story.

Don't Rain on My Parade

Procedure: Each student chooses an occupation to mime. When the pantomime ends, another student acts out a kind of weather that is most advantageous or detrimental to that occupation.

Note: This exercise allows younger children to see that different weather can be positive or negative, depending on circumstances.
Life Guard;
Bird Watcher;
School Bus Driver.

Fish Gotta Swim, Birds Gotta Fly

Procedure: The class is divided into three groups; each group designs an environment in which each student becomes a member of that environment, i.e., a field with grass, daisies, grasshoppers, ants, birds, etc. The group must dramatize a play demonstrating how eliminating one aspect of the environment affects all other elements.

Note: This game shows the interrelatedness and interdependency of all living things.

Frog Cycle

Procedure: Students research the life cycle of a frog. They then make simple frog puppets (refer to the section on puppetry) and improvise puppet plays about frogs based on their knowledge.

Note: Students can adapt this exercise to the study of the life cycle of any animal.

Involvement Science

Procedure: The teacher guides the students through an Involvement drama on any subject matter dealing with science.

Note: The World of Weather;

American Inventions;

Galileo's World.

Keep It Moving

Procedure: One student volunteers to create a perpetual motion machine by assuming some constant motion. The second volunteer must relate to number one's action and supply a complementary or continuing activity. It is helpful if each volunteer says what part they are playing, i.e., cog. The device continues to build until the entire class is involved.

Note: This exercise helps the students to understand the interrelatedness and the interdependency of the various parts.

The Nature of Nature

Procedure: Each student submits a proverb or saying about nature so the teacher may eliminate possible duplications. The class is divided into groups of four; each group is responsible for acting out a proverb or saying about the weather that the rest of the class must guess.

Note: Red Sky in the Morning, Sailors Take Warning;

When Stars Huddle, Earth Will Soon Puddle;

In Like a Lion, Out Like a Lamb.

Survival

Procedure: The class is divided into half. Half becomes lost on an imaginary walk in the woods, while the other half acts out things of nature while following the teacher's unrehearsed instructions.

Note: The teacher instructs the "lost half" on what to look for and the "nature half" on what to do, i.e. Teacher: "We are lost in the woods and need to find a direction out of here; let's look for the north star" (nature half forms constellation, etc.).

Plant a Garden

Procedure: After the entire class has studied how plants, trees, weeds, etc., grow, they become a "garden," from the planting of the seeds to the first sprout to the full-grown plant.

Note: This exercise can be enhanced by using music and broadened to show how weather affects growth, i.e., The Rites of Spring.

Put It to Good Use

Procedure: The class is divided into groups of five. Each group must choose a scientific invention to enact. After the group has completed its design, anyone may enter the scene as a specific character and use the invention.

Note: Radio;

Phonograph;

Automobile.

Scientists of the Round Table

Procedure: The class is divided into groups of four. Each researches a famous scientist (or a team of scientists) and their contribution; one student from each group portrays the famous scientist (two students are chosen if they choose a famous scientist team). The "scientist" meets in a roundtable discussion moderated by Dr. Science to explain the theory and concept of their contribution/s. The "scientist" must maintain a dramatically consistent character throughout the debate.

Note: Einstein, The Curies, Newton, Galileo, Pascal.

Sell Your Product

Procedure: Each student researches how to make a simple everyday product, such as soap, cosmetics, or candles. They then use a specific "sales" character type to explain and sell their product to the class.

Note: An extension of this exercise would be to have the class experiment (under adult supervision) with and make the various products.

Sideshow Science

Procedure: Each student becomes a sideshow barker demonstrating (in character) an experiment in scientific magic. Other groups may be invited to the sideshow.

Note: Mr./Mrs. Cheapskate Show How to Draw Copper From a Penny;

Mr./Mrs. Vesuvius Make a Chemical Volcano Erupt Before Your Very Eyes;

Mr./Mrs. Frostbite Create a Chemical Snowstorm.

Solar System

Procedure: The class becomes a solar system (sun, planets, and moons), and with the teacher's help, they chalk out their orbit path on the floor or playground. At the teacher's command, the students move in their paths while the smaller moons rotate around them.

Note: An interesting variation would be to have a student (moon) move around the Earth so that the moon's same side is always facing the Earth.

Voyage Through the Body

Procedure: The teacher guides the students by a magical boat through the bloodstream, explaining how circulation works. Special side trips can be arranged to "points of interest" throughout the body.

Note: Various students can serve as tour guides at multiple points of interest, pointing out the purpose of specific body parts in character, i.e., Dr. Aorta.

Weather or Not

Procedure: Using a classroom-size map of the United States, have the students act out various weather patterns and forces (according to the day's weather map). Have the class show the interaction between different forces and the weather that these forces produce.

Note: In addition to explaining weather patterns, this exercise will also show the students how to understand a weather map and the various types of weather different parts of the country experience.

Puppetry

This section offers the leader enough basic information to incorporate puppetry into the everyday classroom or life experience. This section includes illustrations and instructions to facilitate the making of simple puppets.

The section on puppetry is self-explanatory and easily accomplished by the students with the teacher's assistance. These simple puppets represent different budgetary levels, so even the class or group with limited finances can include puppetry as a teaching and participation aid.

Puppetry offers a superb style of expression. It is an excellent device for introducing students to dramatic style and self-expression. The child or adult who is shy or somewhat withdrawn frequently finds it easier to relate by using (or hiding behind) a puppet. Speech therapists have utilized sock puppets with the addition of a tongue to help with word pronunciation. Puppetry also helps develop character insight and relationships. It is an excellent introduction to learning the structure of a dramatic play.

There is no need to worry about building an intricate puppet stage as stages have been created from old refrigerator boxes or simply hanging curtains across a doorway. One of the beauties of puppetry is the non-necessity of a professionally structured set. A puppet play can happen anytime and anywhere.

Creativity in puppetry emerges from the style of the improvised play. The improvisation allows maximum utilization of the puppet and the operator's imagination. Some plays are included merely to serve as guidelines for the teachers. Older students can write their own plays, memorize lines, and create amazing and usually humorous characters. My fourth-grade teacher had us improvising plays on American history that provided heightened interest in the subject matter. She read various scripts to us so we would have an understanding of dialogue but allowed us to improvise with only a sequential guideline. We could even go further by scripting the plays for production. This activity kept many of us who often had trouble focusing on even simple tasks very motivated.

The plays in this section are often a mix of comedy and slapstick, with "bits" of history adjusted to keep the audience interested.

Some basic instructions and guidelines are included at the end of the puppetry section and should be carefully considered before determining how detailed you want your puppet to be. Are you doing it for a learning experience for just your students or as informative material for others? My college students often chose informative material connected to a known folk tale because they felt an ethical moment was needed to give a more educational tone to a comedic piece.

Puppets Made Easy

This section offers enough basic background information to incorporate puppetry into the everyday classroom experience. Pictures, patterns, and examples to facilitate the making of puppets are included.

Puppetry is the age-old folk art found in all four corners of the globe.

Shadow and Bunraku Puppets

Puppetry can be as simple in theory as the Indonesian Wayang Shadow Puppets,

where a single operator can create full-length plays for a summer's evening entertainment or, as complex as the famed and ancient Bunraku Puppet Theatre of Japan, where three operators manipulate a single puppet to the

accompaniment of a samisen (musical stringed instrument) and an "actor/reader."

Speech therapists have found a new teaching aid by utilizing a sock puppet with an added tongue to correct speech difficulty with pronunciation. It is an enjoyable way of doing repetitive exercises. Anyone with a bit of imagination and some fundamentals can be a puppeteer. This chapter provides some sample ideas for creating and expanding the art into a simple production.

Learn Thru Play

Household Object Puppets

These puppets, made from household (or found object) puppets, can provide an inexpensive, rainy-day activity for children of all ages. The following pages contain just a few examples of items that can be used to make puppets.

If you look around your home or classroom and let your imagination roam, you will find many more objects that can become puppets. You will want to ensure the object is not "covered up" but freely utilized, as that is the fun of the exercise.

Milk Carton Puppet

The sample below may be used to make a boxy lion moose, villain, etc. It also makes a fun noise when snapped open and shut. A sock or durable fabric may be attached to the

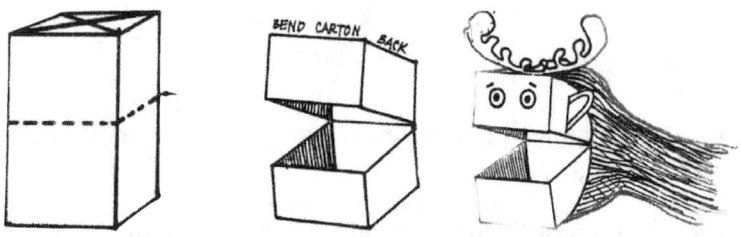

top and bottom to complete the creature. The surface of a milk carton is waxy, so dip the paintbrush over a cake of soap or mix soap flakes into the paint. If this still doesn't help adhere to the paint, you may have to scrape the wax off the carton.

Carrot Puppet

Take a carrot, make facial features and costumes out of paper or felt, and thumb-tack them in place.

Paper Bag Puppets

Empty Bag

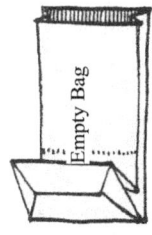  

Use the bag's bottom flap for the features, which may contain eyelids and lashes, thus creating moveable eyes. If the mouth comes at the bottom of the flap, it is more effective for a "mouthy" or fast-talking character.

Stuffed Bag

Stuff the bag with paper towels, newspaper, or lightweight fabric. When the head reaches the desired size, tie it with a string and decorate the face. Use a toilet paper roll for the neck. Make the costume with paper or felt.

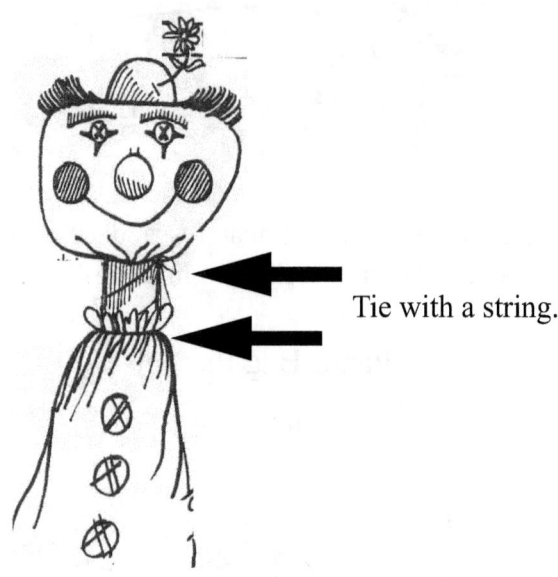

Tie with a string.

Sock Puppets

Take a sock and a broom, either child-sized or regular. Stuff the sock, tie it to the handle and decorate it with felt and

yarn to look like a hobby horse. This can also be a practical device for children to sweep their rooms at camp or home.

The unstuffed sock puppet is easier for younger elementary school pupils.

A Sly Magician

Take an ordinary sock that fits the size of the hand snugly and put it over the hand so the toe fits into your fingers. Open your hand so the space between the thumb and the finger is about an inch on an adult's hand (less on a child's hand), and make a slit in the sock at this point. Next, take a small piece of material- felt is preferred because it won't unravel - and glue or shape it into the mouth area. Then add felt ears, eyes (usually across the knuckle area), yarn hair, wire or pipe cleaner glasses, a hat, or anything to create the puppet's character.

Marionette Style Paper Plate Puppet

An inexpensive and fun way to begin string puppet work is to let the students utilize their imaginations and create characters for a play.

One only needs a few paper plates, brads, a string, and a character idea. Below is a baker, as evidenced by the hat.

Begin by creating a head and a body. Hold two small paper plates face to face. Tie them together with a long string at the center top. Put the two larger paper plates together similarly and brad the smaller plates' bottom to the top of the smaller ones (see sample). Make arms and legs out of construction paper or any lightweight paper and brad to the body as shown.

The brads may need to be adjusted so the arms and legs can be moved to give the character more life.

Hand Style Paper Plate Puppet

Fold a paper plate in half (as shown), staple cloth, or a sock to the top. The folded plate (as shown) is effective as a puppet mouth. Add a decorated sock to become the character the play calls for, and you have a quickly made and practical puppet.

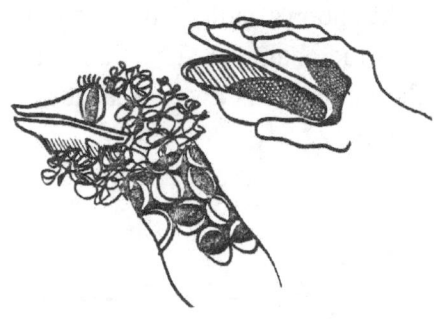

Tennis Ball Style Puppet

A simple base for the moveable mouth hand puppet is created by cutting a tennis ball 2/3rds across the front. The cut will form the mouth of a puppet. When the ball is squeezed, the mouth will move quite effectively. Decorate

the front with magic markers to look like a face and add cloth to hide the hand. This style is most effective as a puppet that talks a lot, i.e., a town gossip, a sports announcer, a side-show barker, etc. The costume may be made from construction paper and stapled or glued to the tennis ball's mouth.

Spoon Puppet

Choose a character to portray and paint features on an old wooden hand spoon's ladle. The addition of a hat or hair may enhance the character. The fun of this puppet style is ensuring the audience is aware that it is a spoon, so don't over-decorate.

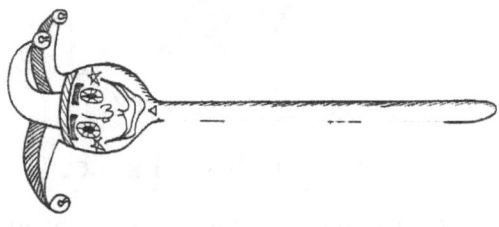

Fly Swatter Puppet

The fly swatter puppet is similar to the spoon puppet because the audience may see the handle. Simple features, such as ping-pong ball eyes and nose, may be wired to the swatter portion of the object to create the character. A small slinky makes an excellent mouth.

Learn Thru Play

Cloth Puppet Animals

Cloth puppets come in many levels of difficulty. For this book, only simple types are utilized because it is an easy task for someone experienced in sewing to create a puppet pattern. Ideally, all puppets should be machine-sewn to make them long-lasting and withstand years of hard usage, but for a beginner who may need to hand sew, hot glue, or stitch wizard their puppet, I have included some samples below to help you get started:

The Dragon Puppet

The dragon puppet is probably the simplest of the fabric puppets.

1. Begin by making a paper pattern. Using your hand as a model, place it palm down on some brown paper and sketch widely around it. This allows for the eventual thickness of your arm. You will want the pattern to go from the fingertips to the elbow joint.

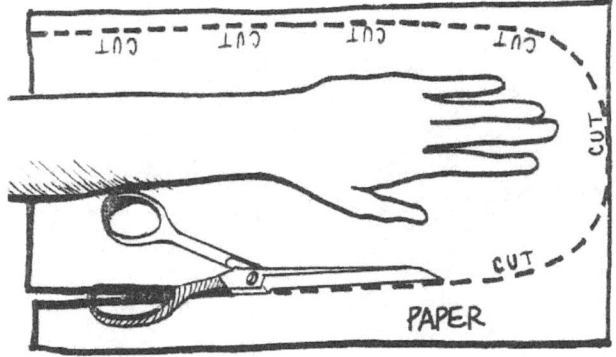

2. Place the pattern on a double thickness of fabric and cut for the puppet's body.

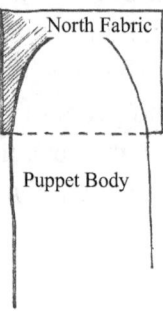

3. Use a separate color fabric for the inside of the mouth. Take the puppet's body and place it on top of the proposed fabric for the mouth, ensuring the mouthpiece is folded over. Cut around the mouthpiece, glue cardboard or stiffener to the wrong side of the mouthpiece, and pin in position,

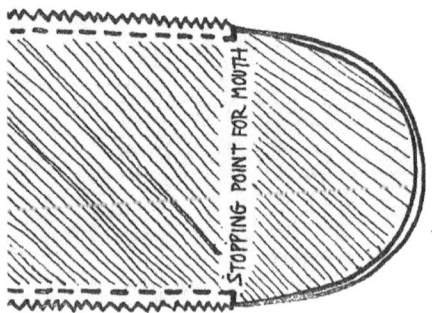

4. Once the mouth is pinned, it is time to sketch out the fine points of your puppet and figure out the placement of the eyes, ears, nose, hair, hat, etc. Ping-pong balls make excellent eyes. This dragon puppet is made from

felt. Although it may only withstand a little wear and tear, it is effective for simple classroom use and easy to decorate.

5. A variation of the dragon puppet would be to create different animals (i.e., frog, dog) by adding legs to the original pattern.

6. A dog puppet made from felt. Notice the placement of the hand for optimum maneuverability.

7. Carefully hand baste, remove pins, and machine sew all the decorations in place. Next, sew the puppet from the back. Sew the mouth in place last.

Costuming Clay, Paper Maché or Styrofoam

Costume for a clay or paper maché head or cut from a styrofoam ball.

A simple costuming method used by my university students is outlined below. It requires more sewing but is more operationally effective due to the perfect fit of the puppet's hands to the operator's fingers.

This method involves cutting three pieces for the body, four separate pieces for the arms and hands, and two for the palm pockets. Sewing as you go makes it less complicated. Simply follow the instructions below for a well-operating puppet.

1. Cut 1 of the Front labeled X and cut 2 of pattern Y. If your hand, when you measure at the neck (top) of the costume, is larger or smaller than 10" plus or minus the seam allowance (usually ½ from the edges) you will need to draw a larger or smaller pattern.

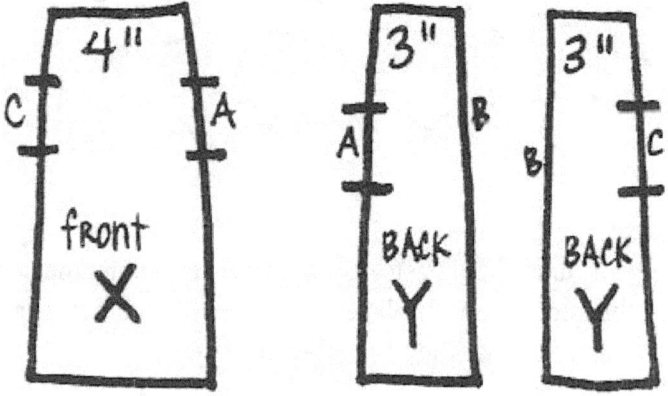

2. Sew Y to Y along line B from the top to the bottom. Then sew Y and Y to X. Leave a space for the arms to be inserted.

3. Make a pattern for the arms similar to the shape of a Z. Ensure the wider part of Z is inserted between the arm

slots on the body labeled A and C.

PLEASE READ THE REMAINING INSTRUCTIONS BEFORE COMPLETING ANY MORE SEWING, AS IT WILL HELP YOUR UNDERSTANDING OF WHAT YOU ARE TRYING TO ACHIEVE.

4. Cut two right and two left hands. Take one right and one left-hand

5. Place one palm piece (a semi-circle that covers the puppet's palm portion of the hand) as shown above left. Place one on the left and one on the right hand. Sew

along the stitching. You now have the bottom of the right and left hands.

6. Attach the remaining hand-pieces to the tops of the correct bottom. Stitch around each finger and down the sides as shown.

7. Next, fill the hands only with quilt-style batting and attach to the BACK of the right and left arms.

8. AFTER the hands are attached to the arms, sew the right sleeve together at the upper and underarm of the body and do the same with the left.

NEARING THE FINISH LINE

9. All that remains to be done is to sew the palm pieces to the costume front. You have created a pocket for your thumb (for your right hand) and pinky (for the right hand) to operate the puppet's hands. Your middle three fingers will be inserted into the puppet's head, allowing for greater maneuverability. If you prefer to operate the puppet with your left hand, make sure you understand the directions before sewing.

10. The costume top may be held around the puppet's neck by a drawstring or elastic located in the neck hem of the costume. Alternatively, the costume may be glued to the neck, but often, the costume may need to be washed, and detaching the costume from a glued neck will be difficult.

Fabrics to Use

Puppets may be made from almost any durable and (preferably) washable fabric. While felt is easy to use for a small school project, it is not a wise choice for puppets that

must be used repeatedly in a show. Felt cannot usually withstand heavy usage and will eventually crumble. Washing too often is detrimental to this fabric.

Heavy cotton, flannel, terry cloth, lighter-weight corduroy, and microfiber blanket fabrics are good choices. No matter what material you use, you want to ensure it is durable and can hide the wearer's hand and arm. For safety's sake, always use nonflammable fabric.

When the puppet is complete, the puppeteer may want to sew a brass ring to the inside bottom of the puppet costume. Plastic rings are available but are less sturdy than brass ones. This added ring allows the puppeteer to quickly slide the ring onto a cup hook (with the Puppet still in hand). The operator may hook the puppet onto a cup hook attached to a backstage wall or to a portable 1x3 that may be carried from location to location and attached to the inside of the touring vehicle for storage.

For marionettes or string puppet storage, it is best to prepare the puppet by holding it from the head cross-bar and then turning the head and body multiple times until the strings are relatively tight. This will prevent the strings from getting tangled. The marionette may then be stored in a giant cloth bag that keeps the lines from unwinding during transportation.

Production Advice

1. The puppet's character must be apparent in their movement and speech styles. For instance, a young, energetic boy such as Jack in *Jack and the Beanstalk* would probably talk and move very quickly, while an older woman would move slowly and talk with a different vocal quality. Remember, only move the puppet that is talking; all other puppets should be in reflective, thinking, or listening poses. This simple rule helps focus the audience's attention on the speaking puppet.

2. The younger students should improvise their lines. Avoid taped conversations because the operators usually become stilted. This makes their performances mechanical and often dull. A story outline will facilitate their improvised dialogue, and rehearsals will bring confidence.

3. People always wonder about the appropriate length of a puppet play. Answers are varied because age is often a determining factor. Ten to twelve minutes is long enough for a single puppet play. Younger children performing will want a show of about six minutes in length. It is important to remember that a small hand puppet is limited in the audience's "attention-holding" ability. The chances of success are thus better if the plays are brief and the story is familiar. A human front-of-stage narrator may also facilitate holding the audience's interest. Clever narration can guide the pace and content of an improvised play.

4. After the group decides which stories to adapt, they should begin designing their puppets. The group must

work together to avoid creating puppets of varying sizes and clashing colors unless called for in the story.

5. Action and comic bits of business are essential in a puppet play. Music, sound effects, and fun songs that highlight character traits are excellent devices to hold an audience's interest and should be used to enhance any production.

Staging Advice

The size of the puppet stage will determine the number of operators and characters that can perform at any given time. Generally, the width of a puppet stage opening is twenty inches per operator. The height is one and a half times the size of the puppet. Portable stages, moved from classroom to classroom, may be about seven feet wide for two or three operators, but care must be taken to ensure the stages may be folded to allow them to go in and out of an open classroom door. To avoid chaos backstage, the teacher may want to limit the number of puppets appearing on stage at one time to three or four.

Handlers often sew curtain rings at the inside bottom of each puppet's costume so the puppet waits upside down on a backstage, nearby cup hook when not in use. The handler may then put their hand directly into the puppet's costume, slide it off the hook, and quickly make an entrance. It is best if the puppeteers determine the above actions during rehearsals, as backstage can be as complicated as onstage.

Rehearsals should be short, as holding up a puppet is exhausting. The more tired the arm, the lower the height of the puppet becomes. The puppet should always appear visible from the (imaginary) thigh up. The puppet's head should be angled down so the character is talking to the audience and not looking over their heads. The costume of a hand puppet needs to completely cover the operator's hand and arm (up to the elbow). The arm will strengthen during rehearsals, and the puppet will no longer sink during performances.

Puppet Plays for Performance

The following plays are adapted from public domain stories that are part of the work of the "Project Gutenberg Literary Archive Foundation" to preserve literary and other intellectual works.

The plays in the following sections are offered here as a very broadly played comedy style. These scripts are for presentation by older students, actors, or teachers to younger children. Each play includes detailed stage directions within the body of the writing.

Jack and The Beanstalk

This is adapted from a public-domain English fairy tale as an example of "melodramatic" characters and a broad acting style.

The cast of characters:

ACTOR #1:   Gaylord Nasty, a typical "melodrama" villain with a handlebar mustache, and the Beanstalk, a colorful prop who may ad-lib lines to add humor

ACTOR #2:   Jack's Mother, Giantess, and Giant (needs vocal contrast between characters)

ACTOR #3:   Jack

ACTOR #4:   Susie (The Singing Cow)

NASTY:	(ENTERS LAUGHING IN AN EVIL MANNER, RUBBING HANDS TOGETHER) Hello! Is Anybody home? (LOOKING AROUND) Anyone around?
MOTHER:	(FROM OFFSTAGE) Who's there?
NASTY:	It is I (THE MOTHER ENTERS, SEES HIM. SHE GASPS FOR AIR AND QUICKLY FANS HER FACE)
NASTY:	Ahem, it is I (HAND TO MUSTACHE) Gaylord Nasty. And I'm here to collect the rent. (LAUGHS EVILLY)
MOTHER:	Ooooh, (CRIES) can't you give us just a few more days? (HANDS HELD UP AS IF BEGGING)
NASTY:	A few days, a few days, (VOICE RISING TO A LOUD YELL) a few days. (CALMING DOWN BUT STILL ANGRY) Every day I come back, it's a few days. Madam, you have had the last few days in quite a few days.
MOTHER:	(SOBBING MADLY) Sob, ahha, ahha.
NASTY:	Ah, madam, stop. (MOTHER CRIES UNDER THIS) I can't stand to see anyone cry.
MOTHER:	Ahhhaaa, aahhhaa.
NASTY:	Madam;. (SHE CONTINUES LOUDER) QU—III-EE- IET!!!

Learn Thru Play

MOTHER: (SHOCKED AND TAKEN ABACK, SHE HICCUPS) You, you yelled at me. (SNIFFS)

NASTY: I'm sorry. Here, take this (HANDS HER A HANDKERCHIEF) and stop all that infernal sniffling.

MOTHER: Hiccup. Hiccups (BLOWS NOSE WITH A LOUD HONK) Thank you. Here's your handkerchief back.

NASTY: (TAKES HANDKERCHIEF IN DISGUST, LOOKS AT IT) Yuck! (THROWS IT AWAY BACKSTAGE) Yucky.

MOTHER: Please, (BEGGING) just one more day. Jack can go to the market and sell susie, the cow. And then we'll have enough money to pay you the last three months' rent.

NASTY: No. I want the money right here (THROWS TANTRUM) right before me, right now, I say, now, now.

MOTHER: (TRYING TO CALM HIM) Just until tonight, then.

NASTY: Madam, do you know when the banks close tonight?

MOTHER: No, I never have enough money to put in them. Oh, please, (CLUTCHING HIM AND PULLING ON THE HEM OF HIS

	JACKET) Just one more day, then Jack can sell the cow. Please. (CLUTCHES HIM AS HE MOVES AWAY, DRAGGING HER ACROSS THE STAGE)
NASTY:	No, absolutely not. (SHE IS STILL PULLING, BUT HE WRENCHES FREE) Well, I'll tell you what! I won't give you one more day, but I will provide you with twenty-four hours (THEY DO A TAKE TO EACH OTHER AND BACK TO THE AUDIENCE AS THE ACTION OF THE PLAY STOPS).
MOTHER:	(LEAPS INTO HIS ARMS, KISSING HIM WILDLY) Oh, thank you, Mr. Gaylord Nasty.
NASTY:	Let go, hmm, now. (PULLS AWAY AND REGAINS COMPOSURE) Till tomorrow. Haa, ha, ha. (EXITS)
MOTHER:	Oh, dear. Jack, Jack, (HE ENTERS) You have to take Susie to market and sell her.
JACK:	Oh, Mom, not Susie.
MOTHER:	Jack, we have to have money for the rent and food. You must sell Susie, or we will starve. Take her now and hurry home with the money. (SHE POINTS TO TOWN AND EXITS SOBBING)
JACK:	Susie, Susie, come here (COW ENTERS SINGING A FEW BARS OF "If YOU

KNEW SUSIE LIKE I KNEW SUSIE") Susie, come on. I have to take you to the market and sell you so we can pay the rent. (COW MOOS, SADLY) I'll sell you to someone nice, Susie, don't worry. (HE TURNS TO PET THE COW, AS NASTY ENTERS LEFT IN A BAD DISGUISE. JACK AND SUSIE FREEZE)

NASTY: (ASIDE TO THE AUDIENCE) Little do they know that their land contains oil and gold. If I can keep them from paying the rent, I can throw them off, and I'll be rich, rich, rich. Aha. Gold, wealth (JACK AND SUSIE'S FREEZE ACTION ENDS AS NASTY MOVES TO JACK AND PRETENDS TO BE NICE) Aha, my good lad, where are you going with such a fine-looking bovine? (VOICE IS ALA W. C. FIELDS) No, don't tell me. I am a sooth. (HE WAVES HIS ARMS AS IF HE IS SEEING SOMETHING THROUGH A MIST) Your name is Jack, and you're on your way to market to sell your cow, right?

JACK: But how did you know?

NASTY: (JUMPS BACK AND SPREADS ARMS WIDELY AS IF MAGICAL. HIS VOICE BECOMES EERIE) I am a Sooth; I know everything about everybody. You are very poor and need money quickly.

JACK: Ooh, yes. How did you know?

NASTY: Kid, I have a deal for you. I will give you this bag (HOLDS UP BAG VELCRO ATTACHED TO HIS HAND) containing five magic beans. (WAVES THEM IN FRONT OF JACK'S FACE) Remember, five magic beans. These five beans, when planted, will grow and grow (NASTY LOOKS UP AS HE SAYS GROW AND FURTHER UP ON ANY ADDITIONAL GROW LINES. JACK FOLLOWS HIS GUIDANCE) and grow. It will take you right to the top, kid. (HEE HEE) Wealth, fame, and fortune will be yours. Five beans for one cow (HOLDS UP LEFT HAND AS THE FIVE AND THE RIGHT HAND FOR THE ONE; HE KEEPS DOING THIS, AND JACK IS ALMOST HYPNOTIZED), fair enough?

JACK: Well…

NASTY: Listen, kid, do you want them or not? (THIS IS A DROP OF CHARACTER)

JACK: (QUICKLY) I'll take them.

NASTY: (SHOCKED) You'll take them? (SURPRISED BUT CATCHES HIMSELF) I mean, you'll take them!!! Ah, ha, a smart lad: (JACK EXITS AFTER SAYING GOODBYE TO SUSIE)

JACK:	Goodbye, Susie (EXITS). When I'm rich, I'll come and buy you back.
COW:	(SINGING) If you knew Susie like…
NASTY:	(NASTY DOES A DOUBLE TAKE) How now, a singing cow. Do that again.
COW:	If you knew Susie like I knew Susie,
NASTY:	Stupendous. Try it again, and I'll join in,
COW:	If you knew Susie like I knew Susie.
TOGETHER:	(THEY DO A QUICK VAUDEVILLE EXIT, MOM ENTERS)
JACK:	Look what I got for Susie. You'll be so proud! (HOLDS OUT HAND)
MOTHER:	Jack, where's the money? (IN CONFUSION)
JACK:	Mom, I sold Susie for these magic beans. The man said I would go right to the top.
MOTHER:	Beans! What good are beans? They won't pay the rent? Give them to me. (THROWS THEM OUT) Oh, Jack, what will we do? (SOBS AND EXITS WAILING MELODRAMATICALLY. JACK HEARS A MUSICAL SOUND AND LOOKS OVER AT THE LOCATION OF THE BEANS. THERE IS THE BACKGROUND SOUND OF A KAZOO AS THE BEANSTALK GROWS)

JACK: Holy Zounds. Jiminee. Look at the size of that Beanstalk. (HE STARTS TO CLIMB. THIS IS DONE BY LOWERING THE BEANSTALK AS HE GOES UP, WHICH LOOKS AS IF HE HAS REACHED THE TOP) Whew, at last, the top. (LOOKS ABOUT. THE BEANSTALK IS NO LONGER SEEN) What a strange land. (GESTURES AS HE LOOKS ABOUT) Everything is so huge, Look over there at that castle. (AN ACTUAL CASTLE FLAT IS NOT NEEDED). I better find out where I am. (WALKS IN PLACE AND GRADUALLY REACHES CASTLE AND KNOCKS ON AN IMAGINARY DOOR THAT SUDDENLY APPEARS OFFSTAGE LEFT. THE SOUND OF THE DOOR CREAKING OPEN AS A VERY TALL PUPPET GIANTESS APPEARS).

GIANTESS: Yeees. What can I do for you? (CACKLES AS SHE LOOKS AT JACK)

JACK: Yikes. (HE REACTS TO HER HEIGHT) Pardon me, but.

GIANT: (FROM OFF STAGE RIGHT. LOCATED WHERE THE BEANSTALK WOULD HAVE BEEN A LOUD VOICE IS HEARD) Fee Fi Fo Fum-

JACK:	(LEAPING INTO GIANTESS'S ARMS) What was that?
GIANTESS:	My son. He's a fierce giant who makes meals of little boys like you.
JACK:	(FALLS FROM HER ARMS AND GRABS THE HEM OF HER APRON, BEGGING) Oh, please, don't let him hurt me. You've got to save me. I have to return to my mother. Please help me.
GIANTESS:	Well. (LOOKS AT HIM CAREFULLY AND BEGINS TO CACKLE) You remind me of my son when he was younger and smaller. I'll hide you, and when the giant falls asleep, you must run home.
JACK:	Oh, I will, I will.
GIANTESS:	Here, over here, behind the wood pile. (HE HIDES OFF STAGE LEFT)
GIANT:	(ENTERING WITH A BAG OF GOLD OVER HIS SHOULDER) Fee Fi Fo Fum. I smell the blood of an Englishman. Be he alive or be he dead, I'll crush his bones to make my bread. (SNIFF SNIFF) I smell something. (LOOKS AROUND) Well?
GIANTESS:	Oh, don't be absurd. That was last night's supper. Now, sit down and count your gold. It will keep you from getting hungry.

GIANT:	(HE PUTS HIS BAG OF GOLD DOWN) Mother, bring my goose that lays the golden egg. (SHE RUSHES OFF TO DO HIS BIDDING AND RETURNS. AS THIS BIT OF BUSINESS GOES ON, SHE BECOMES MORE AND MORE TIRED WITH EACH TRIP) Now, bring my singing harp. I want some music. (SHE RUSHES OFF AS THE GOOSE, WHICH IS A PUPPET THAT ACTOR 2 OPERATES, NIBBLES THE GIANT'S ARM, AND THE GIANT AD-LIBS. THE GOOSE AND EGG MAY BE MADE OUT OF POSTER BOARD OR JUST PICTURES GLUED TO A STICK. THESE ARE EASILY OPERATED BY ONE PERSON FROM BACKSTAGE).
GIANT:	Gold and wealth are all mine. Ho Hum, (SNIFF) I still think I smell a human. Oh, well, I'm tired. Yawn. Sleep (HIS HEAD FALLS OVER TO HIS CHEST, AND HE SNORES LOUDLY).
JACK:	Now's my chance. (GRABS GOLD, RUSHES TO THE EDGE OF THE BEANSTALK AND THROWS THE BAG DOWN) Now, for the goose and the golden harp. (HE GRABS THEM UNDER HIS ARM, AND AS THEY START TO DESCEND THE BEANSTALK, THE BEANSTALK GROWS IN HEIGHT, SO IT APPEARS JACK IS GOING DOWN THE STALK

	WITH THE GOOSE AND THE HARP. THE GOOSE MAKES LOUD NOISES) Shh, quiet, will you? Now, how am I going to get down this Beanstalk with them? (HE STARTS DOWN AS THE GIANT WAKES UP)
GIANT:	What's that? My gold, my goose, my harp. Where are? (SEES JACK) Ah ah, ah, I'll get you.
	(THE GIANT RUNS ACROSS THE STAGE AND MAKES A FLYING LEAP. HE GOES OFFSTAGE. JACK IS AT THE BOTTOM OF THE BEANSTALK AS THE GIANT MAKES HIS FLYING LEAP, THE STALK LEANS TO STAGE LEFT AND SHAKES A LOT)
JACK:	Mother, get the axe, the axe.
MOTHER:	(ENTERS WITH AXE) Here it is. (CHOP CHOP SOUNDS AS JACK CUTS DOWN THE STALK. THE GIANT MAKES A FALLING SOUND (aghhh). A KAZOO MUSICALLY DESCENDS THE SCALE AS THE GIANT FALLS OFFSTAGE. IT WILL BE NECESSARY FOR THE ACTOR PORTRAYING NASTY AND THE GIANT TO SPEAK THE DIALOGUE WHILE ANOTHER PUPPETEER IS THE PHYSICAL HANDLER. AS SOON AS NASTY AND THE GIANT HAVE

	FALLEN AND ROLLED OFFSTAGE, EVERYONE CAN MOVE TO THE FINALE. THIS SWITCHING OF ROLES AND HANDLING OF PROPS WILL REQUIRE SOME ADDITIONAL REHEARSAL TIME)
NASTY:	(ENTERING) Ah, time to get the rent.
	(LOOKS UP AS JACK YELLS)
JACK:	Here she goes. (JACK SEVERS THE BEANSTALK. THE GIANT OR THE STALK FALLS ON TOP OF GAYLORD NASTY AND SQUASHES HIM TO THE GROUND)
NASTY:	Foiled again. (SPLAT) (THE COW RETURNS TO HUGS FROM MOTHER AND JACK. THE SHOW MAY END HERE BUT IS RICHER WITH THE ADDITION OF A SONG IN THE PUBLIC DOMAIN. JACK, HIS MOTHER, AND THE COW DANCE ABOUT. THE CHOSEN SONG MUST BE AGE-APPROPRIATE. IT CAN HAVE RE-WRITTEN WORDS AND BE TAUGHT TO THE AUDIENCE OR JUST SUNG AS WRITTEN BY THE CAST WITH THE AUDIENCE INVOLVED)

To Philadelphia

To Philadelphia is a play that students may perform or use as a suggestion for other puppet productions with historical significance. The song "Yankee Doodle Dandy" is in the public domain and was often sung by the colonists during the Revolutionary War. Those with musical or lyrical talent may write new lyrics or add a small orchestration to the song. It may also be used as a finale to the show.

This play has been successfully performed with as few as three actors. The Narrator remains the narrator throughout. Actor #1 plays Della, Rhoda, and Sir, and Actor #2 plays Newton and Brim.

The cast of characters:

ACTOR #1	Delawicious (Della) Donkey has a braying and terrible singing voice;
ACTOR #2:	Rhoda is a determined chicken with a clucking voice like an angry bird;
ACTOR #3:	Newton J. Hound. He is also known as Newshound, a Basset or hunting-style puppet with his nose to the ground;
ACTOR #4:	Sir, a pompous British Major General;
ACTOR #5:	Brim, a gullible British soldier;
ACTOR #6:	Narrator, non-puppet.
NARRATOR:	(ON THE SIDE OF THE PUPPET STAGE) Back in Colonial America, at the

beginning of our new nation, some very unusual characters became involved in the struggle for independence.

NEWTON: (POPS UP SNIFFING AT NARRATOR)

NARRATOR: Newton, what are you up to?

NEWTON: Newton J. Hound here, (SALUTES) news reporter extraordinaire. I've got a natural nose for news. Ha ha. (SNIFFS AROUND, PAUSES, LOOKS AT AUDIENCE) I remember one of the finest stories.

NARRATOR: Is it a new story or an old one?

NEWTON: Older, much older. It happened 1775.

NARRATOR: Ahh, I know that one. Why don't you let me do the Storytelling? (PATS NEWTON ON THE HEAD)

NEWTON: (LOOKS AT AUDIENCE AND NARRATOR AND SMILES) O.K.

NARRATOR: (LOOKS AT AUDIENCE, CLEARS THROAT) It was a balmy day in 1775. As usual, Newton J. had his nose to the ground, hunting up news. (SINGING HEARD OFFSTAGE FROM DONKEY - NEWTON SNIFFS OVER - DONKEY APPEARS) Then suddenly, Delowicious donkey appeared. (NEWTON SMELLS DELLA) I think I smell a story.

(THEATRICAL TAKE TO AUDIENCE AND BACK TO DONKEY)

NEWTON: How do you do? Newton J. Hound here. I was in the area looking for a human interest story or animal, as the case may be, and I happened to stick my nose into your predicament. (ASIDE TO AUDIENCE) That's a journalistic expression. (BACK TO DONKEY) Tell me, just what's the story?

DELLA: Really, I ask you, did you ever hear a finer singing voice? Listen to this (LOUD AND BRAYING) I'm a Yankee doodle donkey, a Yankee doodle do or die.

NARRATOR: (FINGERS IN EARS TO SHUT OUT DELLA'S SINGING)

RHODA: Cock a doodle doo. (ENTERS) What's all this racket? I'm trying to rest up for my long journey to Philadelphia. (DELLA AND NEWTON LOOK AT EACH OTHER IN CONFUSION AND SHRUG) Haven't you heard the news?

NEWTON: (SNIFFS) News? And I missed it! (VERY UPSET)

RHODA: A man just rode by yelling that the British are coming, The British are coming. To arms, to arms. Well, I couldn't help him; I don't even have arms, just wings.

(COCK-A-DOODLE, DOO FLAPS WINGS)

NARRATOR: But then, why are you going to Philadelphia?

RHODA: The colonies will fight for independence, and we must take a stand! (SHE MOVES ABOUT FROM NEWTON TO DELLA AS SHE DELIVERS EACH LINE) No taxation without representation. Give me liberty or give me death. I'm off to Philadelphia. (SHE LOOKS AT EACH) Why not come along?

NEWTON: O.K. We'll join you on your march to Philadelphia and tell everyone along the way what's happening. We'll be the troubadours of freedom. (THEY EXIT HUMMING YANKEE DOODLE)

NARRATOR: Suddenly, two British soldiers appeared. (THEY MARCH ON) One was obviously the leader.

SIR: (HE HAS A PROPER BRITISH ACCENT) Brim, bring me the orders.

BRIM: (LOUDLY IN A COCKNEY ACCENT) Yes, Sir, I have them right here. (LOOKS EVERYWHERE AND FINALLY HOLDS UP A PIECE OF PAPER WHICH HE HANDS TO SIR) The orders for the day, Major, Sir. (BRIM

	SAYS THE LAST LINE LOUDLY AND GIVES A SALUTE)
SIR:	(VERY STUFFY WITH A REFINED BRITISH ACCENT) Brim, Lower your Voice. There are colonial spies everywhere. We British must stop those rabble-rousers in Philadelphia. Hancock, Adams, Franklin - why we'll hang them from their own liberty trees.
BRIM:	Isn't that bad for the trees, Sir? What about ecology, Sir?
SIR:	(YANKEE DOODLE IS HEARD IN THE BACKGROUND) What is that noise?
NARRATOR:	At that point, our troubadours came into view. They were unaware of the British soldiers.
SIR:	Halt! Who are you?
NARRATOR:	Trapped and confused, the three hemmed and hawed. (THE PUPPETS VERBALIZE IN CHARACTER VOICES HEM, HEM, HE HAW)
RHODA:	(FLAPS HER WAY TO SIR) Well, you see, Sir (SIR REACTS TO HIS NAME BUT RECOVERS QUICKLY) we are on our way to Philadelphia to um, um, join up with the James Sharp high rider circus.
NARRATOR:	Boy, that was quick thinking.

BRIM:	A real circus with tightropes, jugglers, lions, tigers, and bears? (ALA THE WIZARD OF OZ) Oh my!
SIR:	Brim, contain yourself. (HE THINKS) I'm sure King George would promote me to General if I brought him back circus performers. Brim, lock them up while I arrange to get on the next ship to England. (EXITS)
BRIM:	O.K., you three. Come on. Do you really do circus stuff?
RHODA:	We'll show you our performance before Sir gets back. It's sort of a special performance just for you. (SHE FLAPS HER WINGS)
BRIM:	Wow!
RHODA:	But, to do that, we'll need some costumes.
DELLA:	Costumes?
NEWTON:	(CATCHING ON TO RHODA'S IDEA) Yes, costumes. We'll need a straw hat, a red wig, and a top hat.
BRIM:	Where am I going to find them?
RHODA:	You'll think of something, you intelligent officer. (BRIM SHOWS GREAT PRIDE)
BRIM:	O.K., I'm off. (EXITS)

NEWTON: Now, here's the plot. When he returns with the costumes, we'll disguise ourselves and escape.

BRIM: Here's the straw hat - You (TO NARRATOR) help them with these things. (NARRATOR HELPS THEM PUT THINGS ON, AD-LIBS)

BRIM: The wig. (EXITS AND REAPPEARS).

BRIM: The top hat. Now when can I see your show?

NEWTON: In about four and a half minutes, we must rehearse first.

BRIM: Oooh, that long. Sir will be back any minute.

DELLA: Tell you what, officer, you go and look for him and tell us when you see him coming.

BRIM: O.K., but please hurry. I want to attend the big event. (EXITS)

NEWTON: Ready? (ALL HAVE HATS ON) We're outa here. (THEY DASH OUT WITH A WHISH SOUND)

BRIM: (ENTERS QUICKLY SHOUTING IN THE STYLE OF THE BRITISH ARE COMING) Sir is coming, Sir is coming. Why, where are they? (SCRATCHES HEAD AND LOOKS DIRECTLY AT

	AUDIENCE) My, what talent! They do magic too. They've disappeared!!
SIR:	(ENTERS AND LOOKS AROUND) Brim, (BRIM STRAIGHTENS UP AND SALUTES WHEN HIS NAME IS CALLED) You've let them escape. (BRIM'S HEAD DROPS IN SHAME) After them! (CHASE ENSUES WITH DIFFERENT CHARACTERS POPPING UP AND DOWN. THE MAJOR FINALLY STOPS. HE IS OUT OF BREATH)
SIR:	Forget it, Brim, we'll never catch them.
BRIM:	A rolling stone gathers no moss.
SIR:	Brim, where did you hear that?
BRIM:	From a man named Poor Richard, (BRIM STRAIGHTENS UP) Sir.
SIR:	(YELLING) Brim, that's Ben Franklin's pen name. You've been reading enemy propaganda. (BRIM LOOKS AT SIR AND EXITS RUNNING. SIR RUNS AFTER HIM)
NARRATOR:	(LOOKS AROUND AND WHISPERS) O.K., all clear. Come on.
NEWTON:	That was a close one.
DELLA:	But it worked well.
RHODA:	We'll have to remember that circus ploy.

NEWTON:	And now to Philadelphia.
RHODA:	To Philadelphia.
DELLA:	To Philadelphia.
	(THEY SING "YANKEE DOODLE DANDY," IMPROVISE A LITTLE DANCE, BOW, AND SAY)
ALL:	The end.

Learning History In A Fun Way

The "History" play is geared at getting the students interested in combining well-known folk tales with historical moments. *To Philadelphia* is based on the famous *Town Musicians of Bremen.* It is part of the public domain Brothers Grimm collection. The puppets may be household object style or made of cloth with movable mouths and hands.

The cloth puppets with two hands allow the puppeteers to show more "expressions" and, on occasion, will enable them to hold various objects. The puppeteer has the thumb in one of the puppet's hands and the pinky finger in the other. The remaining three fingers will move the puppet's mouth up and down. This maneuver takes a lot of practice, but the operation is more effortless if the puppet's mouth is reinforced with buckram (a stiff fabric).

Story Theatre

There are many books on Storytelling but few on Story Theatre, a form that Paul Sills developed in the late 1960s. Improvisational in its initial state, a more scripted form titled *Story Theatre* reached Broadway in the 1970-71 season.

In storytelling, a single storyteller takes on various characters' narration and dialogue. Story Theatre is a more theatrical and physical form with multiple actors portraying different characters. To allow the reader to understand the style of this art form, bits of "theatrical business" have been included in the following scripts. The aim is to help teachers, leaders, directors, and actors visualize the final product by focusing on the story, characters, and stylized comedy. In some ways, it is similar to Commedia Del'Arte and Moliere.

Story Theatre is the perfect outgrowth of storytelling. It most often involves a small cast that plays many roles and often represents props, such as a table or a door. Performing in this style is an actor's delight and an excellent way to explore broad slapstick comedy. Usually, the actors will play multiple roles in the same play. Thus, physicalizing a character's personality trait is essential so the audience will know which character the actor is portraying.

One person may handle narration throughout, or it may switch among actors, but this is clear to an audience because the actors will have an indistinguishable style when they are the various narrators, i.e., similar vocal pacing. The narrative is critical to this theatre style. The advantage of Story Theatre is that it has no real need for props or costumes and sets, so it has the flexibility of performance space. The actors often have one neutral costume, i.e., colorful overalls and a shirt.

Educationally, it allows the student audience to see literature come alive. The actors are illustrators of the words. The audience develops an increased awareness of character and plot, which hopefully will also increase a desire to read or to adapt stories, portions of novels, or poems to theatre performances.

The scripts included here show how a small cast can portray many parts. Any teacher or group leader can combine some exercises from the "Games Section" and, with the addition of a work of poetry or literature, create their own Story Theatre play for performance.

Middle Schoolers will enjoy adapting their own public-domain folk tales. Any folk, fairy tale, poem, or historical moment can be adapted into a Story Theatre presentation.

I taught various college students how to find, script, act and direct Story Theatre plays. As they became more enamored of the genre, we worked together to add bits of business and broaden the original style to capture various difficult and different age audiences in outdoor and indoor spaces. Over the years, it became apparent that this was an excellent training ground for anyone desiring a venue for honing one's comic skills, either as an actor or director.

In looking for possible stories to adapt, "The Gutenberg Project" is an online library of works in the public domain and an excellent resource for "kicking off" a unit in Story Theatre. This is also an excellent opportunity to include diverse stories from different cultures.

Sample scripts in this text contain materials designed for a humorous, broadly stylized, slapstick approach to performing. The company must always handle this material sensitively to avoid crossing the line from comic slapstick into violence. More often than not, classic folk and fairy tales contain a "nasty" or villainous character. Although the included scripts preserve this "evil" quality, the tone is humorous. In miming physical activity for the traditional downfall of the villain, these matters focus on stylized comedy rather than hitting or fighting.

Learn Thru Play

Paul Revere's Ride

Story Theatre for three actors. I have directed it with fewer performers, but it is easier with three. This is an example of how poetry and history may be enhanced. Since this is an adaptation of the famous Longfellow Poem, The leader may want the actors to explain why Longfellow chose Revere as the title character. He was captured while the other riders were not.

The cast of characters:

ACTOR #1: Narrator

ACTOR #2: Paul Revere

ACTOR #3: A variety of characters

Properties are needed to add to the humor and help the audience focus and retain dates and sequences. They include a large clock with moveable hands that the narrator changes as Paul rides through the night. A two-sheet "day date calendar" reading April 17th, 1775, with April 18th under it. The April 17th will be removed as part of the "business" and story.

NARRATOR: Listen, my children, and you shall hear of the midnight ride of Paul Revere. (HOLDING TWO SHEETS OF A SINGLE-PAGE CALENDAR. THE DATE APRIL 17, 1775, COVERS APRIL 18, 1775. THE NARRATOR PLACES THEM ON A MUSIC STAND OR A

(STANDING PROP WITH A HOOK, OR A BULLETIN BOARD. THE CLOCK MAY ALSO BE PLACED ON THE BOARD AT THIS MOMENT OR WAIT UNTIL THE NORTH CHURCH SECTION)

(PAUL ENTERS AND MIMES AS IF RIDING A HORSE WHILE MAKING CLIP-CLOP HOOVE SOUNDS. HE CROSSES THE STAGE, GIVES THE NARRATOR A DIRTY LOOK, AND RIPS THE NUMBER 17 DATE OFF THE CALENDAR TOP, SO IT NOW READS APRIL 18, 1775. HE GLARES AT THE NARRATOR)

NARRATOR: (LAUGHS NERVOUSLY AND LOOKS SHEEPISH. PAUL EXITS STAGE LEFT) On the eighteenth of April, in Seventy-Five; Hardly a man is now alive Who remembers that famous day and year

ACTOR #3: (ENTERS STAGE LEFT AS AN ELDERLY PERSON MUTTERING) I remember, I remember. (EXITS STAGE RIGHT)

(NARRATOR REACTS TO ELDERLY PERSON).

(DURING THE NEXT NARRATIVE, PAUL ENTERS STAGE LEFT, ACTOR #3 ENTERS STAGE RIGHT, AND

Learn Thru Play

WITH THEIR BACKS TO EACH OTHER THEY SLOWLY WALK AND LOOK SIDE TO SIDE. THEY REACT IN SURPRISE AS THEY MEET BACK TO BACK IN THE MIDDLE. ACTOR #3 BECOMES PAUL'S FRIEND ON THE LINE BELOW, AND THEY WALK DOWNSTAGE TOGETHER)

NARRATOR: He said to his friend. (ARM AROUND PAUL'S SHOULDER AS THEY WALK DOWNSTAGE)

PAUL: If the British march (THEY BOTH MARCH IN PLACE ON THE WORD MARCH) by land or sea (ON THE WORD LAND THEY BOTH HOLD THEIR HANDS FLAT AND STILL AND ON THE WORD SEA THEY DO A WAVING OCEAN GESTURE) from the town, tonight, hang a lantern aloft in the belfry-arch (MIME HANGING LANTERN) of the North Church-Tower, as a signal light, one if by land (HOLDS UP INDEX FINGER), and two (HOLDS UP TWO FINGERS) if by sea; (#3 REPEATS PAUL'S GESTURE OF ONE AND TWO) And I, on the opposite shore will be,

Ready to ride and spread the alarm

Through every Middlesex Village and farm,

	For the country - folk to be up and to arm.
NARRATOR:	Then he said.
PAUL:	Good -night.
NARRATOR:	And with muffled oar,

> (PAUL LEAPS INTO AN IMAGINARY BOAT AND QUICKLY CROUCHES AS IF SITTING AND BEGINS ROWING, SPEAKING AS HE SAYS) muffle, muffle, muffle

Silently row to the Charlestown shore,

> (PAUL GIVES A SSHH MOTION TO HIS LIPS AS HE ROWS).

Just as the moon rose over the bay,

> (ACTOR #3 BALLET STEPS ACROSS THE STAGE, ARMS IN A CIRCLE AS IF HOLDING A BIG MOON)

Where swinging wide at her moorings lay

The Somerset, British man-of-war:

A phantom ship, with each mast and spar

Across the moon, like a prison-bar,

And a huge, black hulk, that was magnified

By its own reflection in the tide.

NARRATOR:	(LOOKS AT IMAGINARY REFLECTION IN THE WATER AND SCREAMS IN FEAR. PAUL MAKES A SSSHH MOTION AND ROWS OFF STAGE. THE ACTOR IS STILL JUMPING ABOUT WHEN #3 COMES ON AND SAYS) Ahemm.
NARRATOR:	Oh, (haha), excuse me. Where was I? Oh yes.
	(ACTOR #3 HOLDS IMAGINARY LANTERN ALOFT AND POINTS AT SELF) Meanwhile, his friend, through alley and street (ACTOR #3 MIMES ACTION I.E. PULLS EARS, HOLDS HAND TO EAR ETC.)
	Wanders and watches with eager ears
	Till in the silence around him he hears
	The muster of men at the barrack-door,
	The sound of arms, and the tramp of feet,
	And the measured tread of the grenadiers.
ACTOR # 3:	(PULLS OUT TAPE MEASURE AND TRIES TO MEASURE TRAMPING FEET)
NARRATOR:	(STAGE WHISPERS TO ACTOR #3 TO GET ON WITH IT AND TAKES TAPE MEASURE) Marching down to their boats on the shore.

NARRATOR:	(ACTOR #3 FOLLOWS MARCHING, THEN TURNS AND MIMES ENTERING CHURCH AND CLIMBING)
	Then he climbs to the tower of the Old North Church. Up the wooden stairs (ACTOR #3 MIMES CLIMBING THE STAIRS AND STOMPING LOUDLY TWO AT A TIME)
	With stealthy tread (ACTOR #3 CALMS DOWN AND GETS STEALTHY)
	To the Belfry-chamber overhead
	And startled the pigeons from their perch
	(ACTOR #3 REACTS AS IF PIGEONS ARE ATTACKING AND ALMOST FALLS, MIMES HANGING FROM THE BELL AS THE NARRATOR CONTINUES)
	On the somber rafters that round him
	made masses and moving shapes of shade
	By the trembling ladder, steep and tall.
	(ACTOR #3 LOOKS UP - LOOKS DOWN AND SHAKES HEAD ANXIOUSLY)
ACTOR #3:	(STAGE WHISPER) I'm not going up there.

NARRATOR:	You have to -
ACTOR #3:	Why?
NARRATOR:	It's in the poem.
ACTOR #3:	I don't care; you go up.
NARRATOR:	(LOOKS UP, LOOKS DOWN, LOOKS AT ACTOR #3) For history?
ACTOR #3:	For history?? (THINKS A MOMENT) I'll do it!! Anything for history. (BEGINS CLIMBING; NARRATOR LOOKS RELIEVED)
NARRATOR:	By the rambling ladder, steep and tall
	To the highest window in the wall
	Where he paused to listen and look down
	(ACTOR #3 LOOKS AND STARTS TO FAINT, COVERS EYES WITH HANDS AND PEEKS OUT BETWEEN FINGERS).
	A moment on the roofs of the town,
	And the moonlight flowing over all (ACTOR #3 EXITS ON THE MOONLIGHT LINE USING BALLET MOVES)
	Beneath in the churchyard lay the dead,
	In their night encampment on the hill...

PAUL:	(ENTERING OUT OF CHARACTER) THE ACTOR IS IN AN IMPATIENT MOOD) Will you cut the next stanza and get on with it? After all, this is my poem.
NARRATOR:	(NODS QUICKLY TO PAUL. THE NARRATOR SPEEDS THROUGH THE NEXT FEW LINES AS PAUL MIMES THE ACTION).

Meanwhile, impatient to mount and ride

Booted and spurred with a heavy stride

On the opposite shore walks Paul Revere.

Now, he patted his horse's side.

(PAUL LOOKS PERTURBED AS THERE IS NO HORSE. THE NARRATOR WHISTLES AND MOTIONS ACTOR #3 TO PLAY THE PART)

(ACTOR #3 ENTERS) I hate this part (BENDS OVER LIKE A HORSE AND PUTS HEAD UNDER PAUL'S HAND)

Now gaze at the landscape far and near

Then, impetuous, stamped the earth (PAUL STAMPS EARTH)

And turns and tightens his saddle-girth

(TIGHTENS GIRTH AND ACTOR #3 WINCES AND GASPS)

But mostly, he watched with eager search (PAUL MIMES SEARCHING WITH A SPYGLASS)

The belfry tower of the old North Church,

As it rose above the graves on the hill,

(NARRATOR BECOMES THE CHURCH)

Lonely and spectral and somber and still

And lo! As he looks at the belfry's height

A glimmer and then a gleam of light

(NARRATOR BEAMS)

He springs to the saddle, (ACTOR #3 GROANS) the bridle he turns

(NARRATOR YELLS) Wait a minute! (PAUL TURNS BACK)

But lingers and gazes till full his sight

A second lamp in the belfry burns... (NARRATOR BEAMS)

(PAUL STARTS, AND ACTOR #3 YELLS) Speed it up, will you?

(NARRATOR FIDDLES WITH THE CLOCK, POINTING THE HANDS AT MIDNIGHT)

It was twelve by the village clock when he crosses the bridge into Medford town,

He heard the crowing of the cock
(ROOSTER SOUNDS)

And the barking of the farmer's dog
(BARKING)

And felt the dampness of the river fog,
(BRR, COUGH)

That rises after the sun goes down.

(PAUL RIDES BY. THE NARRATOR FIDDLES WITH THE CLOCK, TURNS IT TO ONE)

It was one by the village clock

When he galloped into Lexington

He saw the gilded weathercock

Swim in the moonlight as he passes

(PAUL RIDES BY)

ACTOR #3 Hurry it up, will you?

(NARRATOR TURNS CLOCK TO TWO)

NARRATOR: It was two by the village clock

When he came to the bridge in Concord town

He heard the bleating of the flock
(BLEAT SOUND FROM NARRATOR)

And felt the breath of the morning breeze.

(PAUL RIDES BY ACTOR #3 YELLS)
Faster, faster. Cut to the end.

(IF DESIRED, PAUL CAN BE CARRYING ACTOR #3 WHO IS WHINING AS THE HORSE)

So through the night rode Paul Revere

And so through the night went his cry of alarm

(PAUL YELLS OFFSTAGE) Alarm, Alarm

To every Middlesex village and farm

A cry of Defiance (PAUL YELLS) "De—fi-ance" and not fear,

A voice in the darkness (PAUL YELLS) "To Arms!"

A knock at the door (HAND REACHES OUT WITH KNOCKING MOTION AS SOUND IS HEARD)

And a word that shall echo for evermore (ECHOS ARE HEARD FROM PAUL AND ACTOR #3) "Evermore, Evermore."

For borne on the night-wind of the past,

>Through all our history, to the last,
>
> In the hour of darkness, peril, and need
>
> The people will wake up and listen to hear
>
> The hurrying hoof-beats of that steed (ACTOR#3 ENTERS AND BOWS)
>
> And the mid-night message of Paul Revere (PAUL BOWS)

NARRATOR: The End (BOWS)

Learn Thru Play

Stone Stew

Story Theatre for two.

This play is based on an old folk tale and may be performed by two adults as an introduction to the Story Theatre style. The staged actions make this simple story much more interesting.

The cast of characters:

ACTOR #1: Narrator and suspicious elderly person

ACTOR #2: Vagabond

NARRATOR: Once, there was a vagabond who was slowly walking. (ENTER VAGABOND SKIPPING, HOPPING, AND JUMPING) I said slowly.

VAGABOND: Oh Sorry. (MIMES A SLOW, HEAVY WALK) slowly walking in the forest. The tired and hungry (MIME THE ACTION) vagabond feared there would be no warm shelter that night.

NARRATOR: Suddenly, way off in the distance, a light appeared. (NARRATOR OPENS AND SHUTS HANDS TO IMITATE A BLINKING LIGHT)

Learn Thru Play

VAGABOND: Aha. A warm shelter. A bite to eat and a comfortable place to stay. Knock, knock, knock. (MIME RAPPING ON DOOR AS SAYING THE LINES LOUDLY)

NARRATOR: An elderly person opened the door. (BUSINESS WITH DOOR SQUEAKING OPEN AND GETTING STUCK. THE NARRATOR BECOMES A GRUMPY ELDERLY PERSON)

ELDERLY P: Wha, wha. What do you want? (STILL PUSHING AND PULLING W/DOOR)

VAGABOND: (BREAKING THROUGH THE DOOR) I, your friendly local neighborhood traveler, wonder if I might find a bite and a warm corner to curl up in.

ELDERLY P: No way. I don't let just anyone in here. I'm tired and don't feel like company. And I don't feel like cooking tonight. Go away.

VAGABOND: But I'll be quiet as a mouse. (MIMES BEING A MOUSE WITH MOUSE NOISES)

ELDERLY P: (SHUDDERS) I'm not too fond of mice.

VAGABOND: As faithful as a dog. (GRABBING ELDERLY PERSON'S LEG, HOWLING, PANTING, AND BEGGING)

ELDERLY P: (SHAKING DOG OFF LEG) Enough! You can stay over there in the corner. (IN

Learn Thru Play

A COMMANDING AND LOUD VOICE) Just don't bother me.

NARRATOR: The vagabond knew better than to push, so she waited calmly. After a short time, she started humming and then singing short snippets of food songs. (YES, WE HAVE NO BANANAS, YOU DESERVE A BREAK TODAY, PIZZA HUT SONG, ETC.)

The elderly person started to feel hungry (MIME HUNGER PAINS) and said,

ELDERLY P: I'm starving. (LOOKS AT AUDIENCE IN CONFUSION). I don't know why I keep thinking of food.

VAGABOND: (KNOWING LOOK TO AUDIENCE AS SHE SPEAKS SLOWLY) I could prepare a little something in your microwave.

ELDER P: Microwave? None of them new-fangled devices for me. Would you believe an open fire in the hearth?

VAGABOND: Close enough. Now, all I need to prepare the best meal is that large pot of water hanging over that fire.

VAGABOND: The elderly person pumped a bucket of water and dragged it to the fire. (VAGABOND STANDS BACK, WATCHING THE ELDERLY PERSON MIME THE HEAVY BUCKET OF WATER BEING POURED INTO THE

POT OVER THE FIRE). The vagabond reached into her bag and pulled out a medium-sized stone which she turned this way and that -- listened to -- felt -- shook - and nodded to. (AS IF THE STONE IS MAGICAL)

ELDERLY P: What is that, and what are you doing now?

VAGABOND: This? Why this is only the finest stone in the whole world - Watch.

NARRATOR: The vagabond took the stone, carefully dropped it into the pot of water, and began to stir slowly. (MIMES WITH IMAGINARY LONG SPOON)

ELDERLY P: What are you doing?

VAGABOND: Stirring.

ELDERLY P: No, no, what are you making?

VAGABOND: Why stone stew, of course, and fit for royalty. (SNIFFS POT NOW BOILING)

ELDERLY P: Stone stew?

VAGABOND: Stone stew.

ELDERLY P: Stone stew?

VAGABOND: STONE STEW. (YELLING)

NARRATOR: The elderly person thought she'd heard of everything, but this was something new.

Learn Thru Play

ELDERLY P: Stew from a stone, huh? (SLYLY) May I watch?

VAGABOND: No problem, although the stew might be a little thin since I've made five delicate stews from this very stone this week. Even the best stew stone can get a little tired, you know. (EYES THE ELDERLY PERSON CAREFULLY) It's a shame I don't have a bit of flour to thicken it, but never fear; it will be dee - licious.

ELDERLY P: Flour, huh? Weeell, I might have a bit for you.

NARRATOR: She went to the cupboard (BOTH PHYSICALIZE FOLLOWING THE NARRATOR'S DIRECTIONS) pulled out a large amount, and added the flour to the pot as the vagabond continued stirring.

VAGABOND: It sure smells good. It's almost perfect. Only (PAUSES AS IF THINKING) I think I remember adding some (PRETENDS TO REMEMBER) potato. I can't quite remember why, but it sort of gave it an (SNAPS FINGERS AS IF REMEMBERING) unusual flavor.

ELDERLY P: Why, I have a potato in the vegetable patch.

VAGABOND: (SMILING CUNNINGLY) The vegetable patch? Well, if you think so.

Learn Thru Play

NARRATOR: The elderly person opened the door (MIMES THE BUSINESS AS IT IS SPOKEN), trudged outside, got a potato, brought it inside, and gave it to the vagabond.

ELDERLY P: I found one (EXCITEDLY MIMES HOLDING UP THE TREASURED POTATO) right next to the carrots.

VAGABOND: Carrots!!! Good idea. (SLOWLY AND CLEVERLY). We could throw some carrots in.

NARRATOR: The elderly person trudged back outside and returned with the carrots. (MIMES FIGHTING WITH THE DOOR, DIGGING IN THE GARDEN, AND RE-ENTERING WITH A CARROT) Soon, this conversation was repeated - celery, parsley, onion, salt, pepper. (ELDERLY PERSON IS NOW RUNNING ALL OVER THE PLACE)

VAGABOND: Ah, that's just about done and fit for royalty. The only thing that needs to be added is a bit of meat, but...

ELDERLY P: Meat?

VAGABOND: (SPOKEN QUICKLY) It's not really necessary. But a bit of meat and we could invite the king and queen.

ELDERLY P: Well, I'm as worthy of a good meal as a king or his queen. Here, (MIMES

OPENING ICEBOX) I do have a small bit of meat. (PUTS THE MEAT IN THE STEW POT AND TAKES AN ENORMOUS BREATH) That sure smells good; definitely fit for royalty.

VAGABOND: Well, if the king was to arrive, we'd have to set the table. (ELDERLY P PERSON RUSHES AROUND AND MIMES SETTING THE TABLE)

NARRATOR: (SINCE THE ELDERLY PERSON IS ALSO THE NARRATOR, SHE MUST MODULATE THE VOICE SO IT IS CLEAR THAT ONE ACTOR IS DOING TWO DIFFERENT PARTS) Soon, the table had a tablecloth, silverware, plates, butter, cheese, and some fruit. (THE ABOVE IS MIMED BECAUSE THE HUMOR IS IN THE RUNNING BACK AND FORTH AND PRETENDING TO BRING THINGS ON TO THE TIMING OF THE NARRATOR'S SPEECH)

VAGABOND: That's it. It's done, and no finer stew anywhere. We are ready for a feast. Allow me to serve you.

NARRATOR: And they sat down to feast. (THE TWO MIME SITTING AND RUSHING THROUGH THEIR MEAL. THEY MAY AD-LIB, TALK, OR SING A SONG IF THEY CHOOSE)

ELDERLY P: Ah, such a feast, and all from your stone.

VAGABOND:	(LOOKS AT AUDIENCE AND WINKS) Since you have kindly shared your meal with me, let me present my unique stone as a gift.
ELDERLY P:	(GREEDILY LAUGHING AS SHE ACCEPTS THE STONE) Now, I have an inexpensive way to make a feast.
NARRATOR:	The vagabond waved goodbye, and as she walked, she came upon a new stone, picked it up and said,
VAGABOND:	I wonder where I will eat tonight? (LAUGHS. BOTH BOW AND SAY) The End.

The Blind Men and The Elephant

A Story Theatre poem for two.

The following Story Theatre piece is based on an ancient Buddhist parable that dates to approximately 500 BCE. The story has many interpretations, and this theatrical performance may lead to a lively classroom discussion. The interpretation that is most often used is about truth. Each individual perceives a small truth about an object, but one needs to discover the entire truth by examining all the pieces

The cast of characters:

ACTOR #1   Narrator

ACTOR #2   Six different characters

ACTOR #1:   This is a story about six blind men from Indostan who, many years ago, observed a statue of an elephant.

ACTOR #2:   Stop!! How are we going to perform this story? There are six parts to play and a Narrator, and we are only two…

ACTOR #1:   It's simple. You'll be the six men, and I'll narrate.

ACTOR #2:	Six! Do you want me to play six different people? (VERY UPSET) Have you checked your union rule book lately?
ACTOR #1:	(LAUGHS WITH EMBARRASSMENT) Not in front of all these people. Later, (STAGE WHISPER) We'll negotiate later.
ACTOR #2:	Well. O.K. I'll do it, but only if you play the elephant.
ACTOR #1:	Me, an elephant? Why...
ACTOR #2:	(MIMICKING ACTOR #) Aa aa, not in front of these people. We'll negotiate later.
ACTOR #1:	O.K. It was six men of Indostan (ACTOR #2 DOES ALL SIX CHARACTERS IN RAPID SUCCESSION WITH AD-LIBS. THESE SHOULD BE FACIALLY AND PHYSICALLY VERY DIFFERENT TO ADD TO THE AUDIENCE'S INTEREST. IT MAY BE HELPFUL FOR ACTOR #1 TO SAY FIRST, SECOND ETC. AS ACTOR #2 DEMONSTRATES. ACTOR #1 IS ALSO ABLE TO REQUIRE A VERBAL DESCRIPTION, I.E., A PINCHED FACE MAN, A HUNCHED-OVER MAN WITH A LIMP, ETC. AS ACTOR #2 MUST TAKE ON THE CHARACTER LOOK THE NARRATOR DEMANDS). (ACTOR #1 STARTS OVER) It was six

men of Indostan (ACTOR #2 RUSHES THROUGH ALL SIX CHARACTERS)

To learn much inclined who went to see the elephant

ACTOR #2: (YELLS) That's you! (ACTOR #2 SHAPES ACTOR #1 INTO ELEPHANT POSE WITH HANDS AS TRUNK)

ACTOR #1: Each, by observation, might satisfy his mind. The first approached the elephant (ACTOR #2 FOLLOWS DIRECTIONS AND TAKES ON THE ACTION REQUIRED OF THE POEM) And, happening to fall against his broad and sturdy side, at once began to bawl.

ACTOR #2: Bless me! But the elephant is nothing but a wall (MIMES ALONG ACTOR #1.THIS IS USUALLY DONE BY THE MIME STYLE WALL WALK WITH ALTERNATE HANDS SEEMING TO TOUCH THE ELEPHANT BUT IN ACTUALITY NOT DOING SO.)

ACTOR #1: The second feeling of the tusk, cried:

ACTOR #2: Ho! What have we here

So very round and smooth and sharp?

To me, 'tis mighty clear

This wonder of an elephant is very

like a spear. (ON THE WORD SHARP BEGINS TO LICK HIS FINGER AS IF IT HAS BEEN PUNCTURED BY A LARGE THORN - REACTS ACCORDINGLY)

The third (ACTOR #2 BECOMES THE THIRD AND REACTS IN FEAR WHEN IT IS THOUGHT TO BE A SNAKE)

approached the animal

And happening to take the squirming trunk within

his hands, Thus boldly up and spake:

ACTOR #2: I see

ACTOR #1: quoth he (ACTION CONTINUES AS ABOVE WITH ACTOR #2 REACTING AS DIFFERENT PARTS OF THE ELEPHANT ARE DESCRIBED)

ACTOR #2: The elephant is very like a snake.

ACTOR #1: The fourth reached out his eager hand
And felt about the knee

ACTOR #2: What most this wondrous beast is like is mighty plain

ACTOR #1: quoth he

ACTOR #2: it's clear enough that the elephant is very like a tree.

ACTOR #1:	The fifth, who chanced to touch the ear, said
ACTOR #2:	E'en, the blindest man, can tell what this resembles most Deny the fact who can This marvel of an elephant It is very like a fan
ACTOR #1:	The sixth no sooner had begun about the beast to grope Then, seizing on the swinging tail That fell within his scope (ACTOR #1 TURNS AND CREATES A TAIL WITH HIS ARMS)
ACTOR #2:	I see
ACTOR #1:	quoth he
ACTOR #2:	the elephant is very like a rope
ACTOR #1:	And so these men of Indostan disputed loud and long
ACTOR #2:	(ACTOR #2 GOES THROUGH ALL SIX CHARACTERS YELLING ROPE, FAN, SNAKE, ETC)
ACTOR #1:	Stop! We're at the moral of the poem.
ACTOR #2:	Each in his own opinion
ACTOR #1:	exceeding stiff and strong
ACTOR #2:	Though each was partly in the right
ACTOR #1:	And all were in the wrong.

ACTOR #2: So, often in philosophic wars

The disputants, it would seem

Rail on in utter ignorance

of what the others mean

ACTOR #1: And prate about an elephant not one of them has seen!

BOTH: (BOW) The End!

Learn Thru Play

Casey At The Bat

Story Theatre for two.

This requires actors with a good sense of comedy and character physicality (a fun play to mark the baseball season).

Casey At The Bat by Ernest Lawrence Thayer was written in 1883. This poem may be adjusted for one versatile actor who does all the action and narrates. The actor must have a strong energy level, as it is an exhausting example. The story is more easily acted by two performers.

The cast of characters:

ACTOR #1: Narrator, umpire, and pitcher;

ACTOR #2: Casey, Flynn, Burrows, Cooney, and Blake.

NARRATOR: It looked extremely rocky for the Mudville nine that day; The score stood four to two (RUNS TO A WHITEBOARD AND WRITES THE SCORE #4 AND #2) with but one inning left to play (WRITES NUMBER #9 ON BOARD). And when Cooney died at second (ACTOR #2 BECOMES COONEY, RUNS AND COMICALLY MIMES DYING AT SECOND BASE)

UMPIRE:	Out!
NARRATOR:	And Burrows did the same (SAME BIT OF BUSINESS), a pallor wreathed the features of the patrons of the game- (ASIDE TO AUDIENCE) that means they felt ill and turned pale as ghosts.
	A straggling few got up to go, leaving there the rest, with hope which springs eternal within the human breast. For they thought! If only Casey could get a whack at that,
	They'd put even money now, with Casey at the bat.
NARRATOR:	But Flynn preceded Casey, as did also Jimmy Blake
	and the former was a Lulu, and the latter was a cake.
FLYNN:	(FLEXING MUSCLES AS IF PREPARING FOR A FIGHT) What do you mean by that?
NARRATOR:	So on that stricken multitude grim melancholy sat, for there seemed but little chance of Casey's getting to the bat. But Flynn let drive a "single" to the wonderment of all. (ACTOR #2 BECOMES FLYNN, AS HE SWINGS THE BAT HE MAKES A THWAK SOUND AS IF A BALL WAS HIT)

And the much despis-ed Blakey (ACTOR #2 BECOMES BLAKEY) tore the cover off the ball. (ACTOR #2 BECOMES BLAKEY AND MIMES WITH LOTS OF GRR SOUNDS, RIPPING THE BALL COVER OFF-STOPS AND THEN RUNS TO THE BASE)

NARRATOR: (PHYSICALIZES THE UMPIRE GESTURE WITH WHILE YELLING), "Safe!" And when the dust had lifted, and they saw what had occurred, there was Jimmy safe at second and Flynn a-hugging third.

FLYNN: (FLYNN MIMES PICKING UP A BASE AND HUGGING IT),

UMPIRE: (YELLS) Safe!!

NARRATOR: Then from five thousand throats and more there rose a lusty yell; it rumbled through the valley, (NARRATOR ECHOS RUMBLE, RUMBLE, RUMBLE) it rattled in the dell; (NARRATOR ECHOS RATTLE, RATTLE, RATTLE) it knocked upon the mountain, and recoiled upon the flat; for Casey, mighty Casey, was advancing to the bat.

(ACTOR #2 BECOMES CASEY AS HE SWAGGERS SMUGLY TO HOME PLATE, MIMING SWINGING A BAT.

ACTOR PERFORMS THIS AS LINES ARE SAID)

There was ease in Casey's manner as he stepped into his place; there was pride in Casey's bearing and a smile on Casey's face, and when responding to the cheers, he lightly doffed his hat; no stranger in the crowd could doubt 'twas Casey at bat,

Ten thousand eyes were on him as he rubbed his hands with dirt; (CASEY MIMES RUBBING DIRT ON HANDS AND CONTINUES AS THE NARRATOR DESCRIBES THE ACTION) five thousand tongues applauded when he wiped them on his shirt. Then, when the writhing pitcher ground (NARRATOR BECOMES PITCHER AND MIMES THE ACTION) the ball into his hip, (CASEY ACTS THE FOLLOWING DESCRIPTION AS NARRATOR SAYS LINES) defiance glanced in Casey's eye, a sneer curled Casey's lip.

And now the leather-covered sphere came hurling through the air (NARRATOR MAKES "WHISSH WHAP" SOUND) and Casey stood watching it in haughty grandeur there. Close by the sturdy batsman, the ball unheeded sped;

CASEY: "That ain't my style,"

NARRATOR:	said Casey.
UMPIRE:	Strike one.
NARRATOR:	The umpire said.
	From the benches, black with people, there went up a muffled roar, like the beating of the waves on the storm and distant shore. "Kill him! Kill the umpire!" shouted someone on the stand. (NARRATOR DOES VARIOUS VOICES) And it's likely they'd have killed him had not Casey raised his hand. (FROM THIS POINT ON CASEY'S ACTION FOLLOWS THE NARRATION)
	With a smile of Christian charity, great Casey's visage shone; he stilled the rising tumult, and he made the game go on; he signaled to the pitcher, and once more, the spheroid flew; but Casey still ignored it, and the umpire said,
UMPIRE:	Strike two.
NARRATOR:	(VARIOUS VOICES FROM THE CROWD) Fraud! Cried the maddened thousands, and the echo answered fraud. (NARRATOR YELLS "FRAUD" AND THEN RUNS TO BE THE ECHO WITH THE VOCAL INTENSITY FADING AS IF A REAL ECHO)

(CASEY MIMES THE NARRATION)
But one scornful look from Casey and the audience was awed; They saw his face grow stern and cold, they saw his muscles strain, and they knew that Casey wouldn't let the ball go by again.

The sneer is gone from Casey's lips, and his teeth are clenched in hate; he pounds with a cruel vengeance, his bat upon the plate; and now the pitcher holds the ball, and now he lets it go, and now the air is shattered by the force of Casey's blow.

(CASEY IS FROZEN IN STRIKE-OUT POSITION WITH BAT OVER HIS SHOULDER AND HIS LEGS TWISTED; THE NARRATION BECOMES QUITE FLOWERY)

Oh, somewhere in this favored land, the sun is shining bright. The band is playing somewhere, and somewhere hearts are light, and somewhere men are laughing, and somewhere children shout, but there is no joy in Mudville - Mighty Casey has struck out.

The above is a tour de force for two actors, but it may be adapted to include more performers, i.e., the other batters, the umpire, etc.

Involvement Theatre

The following plays fit into a category titled Involvement Theatre. This style allows actors to combine Story Theatre and audience participation in a scripted form, where the actors perform the dialogue and involve the audience in other parts.

Two included plays, *Communications* and *You Were There,* are based on historical events. They were created from subject matter that the author wanted to expand upon while giving insight into various topics. *Communications* combines history with broadly enacted entertainment. *You Were There* is a much longer play, as it was written for a group of actors to spend the day in a Middle School classroom. Thus, it is filled with more detailed subject matter based on the style of a longer time with the group and to re-create the feeling of actually "being there." This play may be used as a more detailed example to assist teachers in writing their own "subject" matter Involvement Plays. Exercises from the Games Section may also be included and "fit" into the overall school day or week-long theme.

The third script, *Movie In The Making,* is designed strictly for entertainment. The plays mentioned above are just examples to show that any topic or subject matter can be adapted for Involvement implementation.

The most essential element to guarantee success is the Control Figure. The role of the Control Figure is to set guidelines, explain operations, give instructions, and maintain a semblance of order. The Control Figure usually has a Control Device, either sound, word, or phrase, that is most effective when it is an outgrowth or integral part of the script and characters. If making a film, the device becomes the director yelling "cut," if on a sea voyage, the device becomes a ship's horn, etc.

At the beginning of the Involvement Play, the Control Figure explains how to use the Control Device "And now I'll show you my magic whistle!" The Control Figure explains to the audience that whenever the Control Device is used, the audience must freeze and wait for instructions. Freezing means that no one can talk or move and must stay frozen until the Control Figure unfreezes them. Refer to the included Involvement scripts to demonstrate how the Control Device and freezing can be implemented.

In Involvement, the audience can be utilized at any point and for any purpose. If a town scene is being constructed, the audience may become the buildings on the street; if a circus is being portrayed, the audience may become the performers, vendors, etc. Additionally, an audience can make sound effects, provide group decisions, determine the direction of the script, etc.

The Involvement action must be verbalized before the action begins so the participants know what to expect and what they are volunteering for. The audience should have the continuity of Involvement to avoid a "jack in the box" effect where the players leave their seats to perform and then return to their seated audience spaces. Often, they can just sit down in place until the section is over and then return from their Involvement spaces to their audience seats.

The material chosen should be worth doing without being too complex so the group can follow it easily. Beginning Involvement should also utilize smaller audience numbers so that the remainder can observe and decide whether it's "safe" to participate.

Because of the movement and action in Involvement Drama, attention should be paid to using non-violent devices. Fight scenes or physical activities in which the participants could get injured must be avoided.

Even with all these instructions, Involvement Theatre is a complex art to master. It requires much trial and error, patience, and a solid sense of humor. Involvement is a technique that the actors/leaders develop through experience and experimentation.

It will take a few trial productions for the principal actors to believe in their ability to utilize the Control Device. Initially, it may seem awkward, but the more the audience and actors become used to it, the easier it becomes. Eventually, it may not be needed; however, knowing that the Control may be utilized if needed is an asset to all participants.

Learn Thru Play

Communications

An Involvement Play For Three Actors

The cast of characters:

ACTOR #1:	Narrator

ACTOR #2:	Pheidippides, Columbus, Bell, Alfred Vail

ACTOR #3:	Isabella, General, Morse, Watson

NARRATOR:	Today, we're going to talk about communications. In caveman times, if somebody was in danger and wanted to let the other people in the village know about the threat, they'd yell like this (EXAMPLE auuuwa OF YELL). When the others heard this, they froze like statues until the danger passed. We're going to try that today. When you hear the threat yell, followed by my saying "freeze," stop where you are and stay frozen until I clap my hands twice. Then, remain quiet to listen to what happens next. Why don't you (TO THE OTHER ACTORS) show them what I mean?

ACTOR #2:	O.K. (SIMULTANEOUSLY)

ACTOR #3:	O.K. (SIMULTANEOUSLY)

NARRATOR:	Please move around and make a lot of noise until you hear the signal. (THE TWO ACTORS DO SO AND FREEZE ON THE SIGNAL. THE NARRATOR AD-LIBS COMMENTS ABOUT THE FROZEN ACTORS, DECIDES THAT THEY AREN'T VERY GOOD AT IT, AND CONFIDES TO THE AUDIENCE)
	They could be more committed at freezing. Why, I bet you could do a much better job. Now, they'll probably think they did an excellent job of freezing, but we know you can do it more effectively. O.K.? I'll unfreeze them. (CLAPS HANDS TWICE AND ACTORS COME TO LIFE)
ACTOR .#2:	Whew, that was hard.
ACTOR #3:	It sure was.
NARRATOR:	These people out here (TO AUDIENCE) have convinced me they can do it better than you, two.
ACTOR .#2:	What? (SHAKING HEAD) Never.
ACTOR #3:	No, we're the champs.
NARRATOR:	Watch them. O.K., (TO AUDIENCE), now wiggle around in your seats and shake your arms. That's good. (FREEZES THEM WITH THE WORD FREEZE)

ACTOR #2: Wow! They are good, but the hard part is still coming. Can they stay that way when they are unfrozen? If they can, then they're the champs. But they'll never stay quiet. Never.

NARRATOR: (CLAPS HANDS AND UNFREEZES AUDIENCE, WHICH SHOULD STAY QUIET; IF NOT, THE EXAMPLE SHOULD BE REPEATED. IT IS IMPORTANT TO TRUST THAT THIS DEVICE WORKS) Today, we're going to tell you about communications. Communication is conveying information from one person to another. In ancient times, communication spread by word of mouth. For example, in the year 490 BC, after the Battle of Marathon between the Greeks and the Persians, the legendary runner Pheidippides was sent from the battlefield twenty-two and a half miles to Athens to spread the word of the Greek victory.

GENERAL: Got to get the word to Athens that we won. (PACING) Got to get word to Athens. (PACES) How am I going to get...?

PHEIDIPPIDES: (RUNS, ALMOST IN PLACE, LEGS HIGH)

GENERAL: Aha! (CALLING) Pheidippides!

PHEIDIPPIDES: That's me, boss. (RUNNING IN PLACE WITHOUT STOPPING THROUGH THE DIALOGUE)

GENERAL: It's a mission of the utmost importance

PHEIDIPPIDES: I'm raring to go, general. (MOVES FORWARD PUMPING, WITH A LEGS HELD HIGH COMICAL LOOK. HE BACKS UP TO ASK THE QUESTION USING THE SAME LEGS HELD HIGH PUMPING MOTION) Where to?

GENERAL: It will put your name in history, Pheidippides.

PHEIDIPPIDES: Oh, boy. (STARTS OFF BUT BACKS UP AGAIN) Where to, where to?

GENERAL: Athens.

PHEIDIPPIDES: Oh, boy, Athens. (RUNS OFF, LEGS HIGH, STOPS, LOOKS AT AUDIENCE, RUNS BACKWARD IN SAME STYLE, STOPS AT GENERAL) Athens! Do you know how far Athens is?

GENERAL: Sure, only twenty-two and a half miles.

PHEIDIPPIDES: (NODS) Yes. That's right. (RUNS OFF, STOPS, LOOKS AT AUDIENCE, RUNS BACKWARD IN SAME PATH)

GENERAL: (ANTICIPATING HIS REFUSAL) Think about it!!! Only twenty-two and a half miles to glory!!!

PHEIDIPPIDES: (THINKS WITH HAND TO HEAD, A BRIEF PAUSE) Yep. Glory awaits! (PHEIDIPPIDES SETS OFF RUNNING THROUGH THE AUDIENCE IN THE STYLIZED RUN. HE GRADUALLY GETS SLOWER AND SLOWER)

NARRATOR: Pheidippides arrived at the marketplace in Athens, delivered his message,

PHEIDIPPIDIS: We won!

NARRATOR: and collapsed from exhaustion. (PHEIDIPPIDES FALLS)

PHEIDIPPIDES: (GASPING FOR AIR) I told him twenty-two and a half miles was too far. (CRAWLS OFF AS THE NARRATOR ATTEMPTS TO COVER PHEIDIPPIDES'S CRAWLING EXIT)

NARRATOR: Well, word of mouth was acceptable, but it didn't always travel long distances very well, so people began writing their messages. But sometimes, kings and queens had secret messages they wanted to be kept from snoopy eyes, so they put their comments in envelopes and developed a personal sealing method. They would melt candle wax on the envelope to seal it, and then they'd take their royal seal, which was sometimes on their royal ring, and dip it into the soft melted wax. Then, they would remove the ring, let the wax cool and harden, and the envelope would be sealed shut. Isn't that right, Queen Isabella? (SHE COMES RUSHING ON)

ISABELLA: Columbus, Columbus.

COLUMBUS: Right here, Your Majesty. (BOWS)

ISABELLA: Are you ready to go to the Indies?

COLUMBUS: Yes, Your Majesty.

ISABELLA: Good, but we have a slight problem. I have a message I want you to deliver, but no one else must know its contents, not even you. I don't have any candles to make wax. What should I do?

COLUMBUS: All these people can be candles. (GESTURES TO AUDIENCE) We'll light all the candles and let them melt until you've enough wax to seal your letter.

ISABELLA: Yes, that seems like a good idea. (ISABELLA AND COLUMBUS GO INTO THE AUDIENCE TO HELP GUIDE THE DEMONSTRATION)

COLUMBUS: Now, everyone, stand up tall, straight, and stiff, like candles. Now, when I count to three, I'll strike my magic match, and you'll begin to feel hotter and hotter. Ready? 1.-.2.-3. (NARRATOR CLICKS FINGERS AND LIGHTS THE CANDLES) Imagine you are a burning candle and feel yourselves getting hotter and hotter. (TIME THE SPEECH TO THE ACTIONS DESCRIBED) Now, slowly, your head begins to melt, and you're hotter and hotter and melting slowly. (AFTER THE GROUP HAS COMPLETED MELTING) There, Isabella. There's your melted candle wax. There you have it, Isabella. (ISABELLA MIMES PUTTING HER RING IN THE SEALING INK AND SEALING THE LETTER) Thanks, everybody.

NARRATOR: We'll jump ahead a few centuries. In the nineteenth century, an American inventor and painter, Samuel Morse, developed the Morse Code, which was a way to transmit language with a system of dots and dashes to send data long distances.

ALFRED VAIL: (ALFRED VAIL ENTERS, RUNNING SIDEWAYS LIKE A VAUDEVILLE PERFORMER SHUFFLING OFF TO BUFFALO. HE CROSSES THE STAGE SAYING) dot dot dot - dash dash - dash. (HE EXITS)

NARRATOR: What's wrong with him?

MORSE: He's using my new code.

NARRATOR: Can you show these people how it works, Mr. Morse?

MORSE: The code is made up of dots and dashes. The dot has a short tap time, three times shorter than the dash. (TO AUDIENCE) Why don't you all try to send a message through yourselves? Your right hand will be the sender, and your left hand will be the receiver (MORSE DEMONSTRATES BY CLASPING HANDS TOGETHER) Let's send the international call for help using Morse code, S.O.S, Save Our Ship. (GUIDE THE AUDIENCE THROUGH THE DOT DOT DOT, THREE TIMES THEN THREE MORE TIMES. ONLY REMEMBER THE DASH IS THREE TIMES AS LONG AS THE DOT. HERE WE GO. DASH, DASH, DASH, AND WE'LL END WITH DOT, DOT, DOT CODE. S.O.S REPEAT THIS UNTIL THEY SEEM TO ACKNOWLEDGE WITH UNDERSTANDING)

NARRATOR: Thank you, Mr. Morse (MORSE EXITS)

NARRATOR: The following popular communication method was patented by Alexander Graham Bell in 1876. It is called the telephone. He'll tell you how it works.

BELL: (COMES ONSTAGE WITH WATSON, HIS ASSISTANT) I'll be a phone, and you (TO NARRATOR) will be the middle circuit. The message will go from my phone through the circuit, that's you, to the other phone in my assistant Watson's room Now, pick up the handle and crank the lever on the wall. (THE ACTION IS MIMED. A VISUAL PICTURE OF AN EARLY WALL CRANK TELEPHONE WILL ENHANCE THE UNDERSTANDING)

BELL: (CRANK SOUND) Ring.

CIRCUIT: Ring.

WATSON: Hello.

CIRCUIT: Hello.

BELL: Watson, come here.

CIRCUIT: Watson, come here.

WATSON: (THE ACTOR HANGS UP THE PHONE AND RUSHES TO FIND BELL). What did you want?

BELL: It worked, Watson, it worked!

There are two possible endings, and both have been used in various productions. If the Involvement has been particularly long for younger audiences, the company may choose to end it here. If the audience is eager to continue, the actors may choose the alternative ending below.

NARRATOR I've got an idea. Everyone get into straight rows. Everyone on this (right) end of each row will be a phone, while everyone on this (left) end will be a phone, and those in the middle will be a circuit. We'll pass a message of one word per row into one phone, traveling down the circuit to the other phone. We'll do that for each row, and at the end, we'll collect each row's words and put them together for the total message.

(THE MESSAGE IS SOMETHING LIKE THE SHOW IS OVER AFTER OUR LAST SONG. IT IS IMPORTANT THAT ALL THREE OF THE ACTORS KNOW THE CHOSEN MESSAGE IN CASE THE CIRCUIT GETS CONFUSED. THE MESSAGE IS GATHERED BY HAVING ACTOR #3 RUN ALONG AND GET EACH WORD FROM THE LAST PERSON IN EVERY ROW. AFTER THE MESSAGE IS GIVEN TO THE AUDIENCE, THE ACTORS CONCLUDE WITH A MUSICAL FAREWELL.

ANOTHER ALTERNATIVE IS TO GIVE A GARBLED MESSAGE AND AD-LIB ABOUT LINES BEING CROSSED, ETC.)

Now, remember. When you get the message, don't say anything more because the circuit will be empty. (THIS MAY OR MAY NOT BE NEEDED. ACTORS JUDGE FROM PREVIOUS EXPERIENCE)

Learn Thru Play

You Were There

An Involvement play for three actors or more, depending on the requirements of the leader.

Three actors may perform the various characters as written, or the teacher may assign a variety of individual roles and have that "troupe" perform the show for a younger class.

The cast of characters:

ACTOR #1:   Van, Sluice, Narrator

ACTOR #2:   Clinton as Narrator and character

ACTOR #3:   DeSenter, Newsboy/girl

SLUICE: (ENTERS SINGING) I've got a mule... (OFFSTAGE WHISTLE IS HEARD, WHICH CAUSES SLUICE TO FREEZE IN AN AWKWARD AND FUNNY POSITION)

CLINTON: (ENTERS) Hi, my name is Dewitt Clinton. Today, we're going back to the year 1817 to Rome, New York, to learn about the beginnings of the Erie Canal. A canal is an artificial waterway connecting two bodies of water. (NOTICES FROZEN ACTOR) What's the matter with you? (REMEMBERS) Oh, frozen (CLAPS HANDS ACTOR

Learn Thru Play

UNFREEZES) My name is Dewitt Clinton, head of the newly formed Erie Canal Commission, and I'm here to tell you how the Erie Canal was built. But first, I have to teach you about this whistle. It's a canal boat whistle used when there may be danger on the canal. So whenever you hear it, everybody has to freeze. We'll give you a demonstration of how it works. (THE TWO DEMONSTRATE HOW THE FREEZE WORKS. IT IS A TECHNIQUE THAT MAY BE USED AS NECESSARY. OFTEN, IT IS NOT NEEDED AT ALL, BUT IT IS BEST TO SET IT UP IN THE BEGINNING AS A CONTROL DEVICE IN CASE THE PARTICIPATING GROUP GETS TOO NOISY OR UNFOCUSED)

And now, back to the show. In the olden days, waterways were the easiest and fastest way to travel. In 1817, America needed a water route from the East to the western frontier, and the Erie Canal was that link. It was a great idea, but plenty of people were against the canal. There was one in particular named DeSenter.

DESENTER: Hi, my name is DeSenter. Now listen here, Dewitt Clinton, we can't possibly pay for this canal. I'd be all for it if you could get the money, but you'll never get it, not in a million years.

CLINTON: There were offers of money from various people. One was from a significant and wealthy person who had much to gain.

VAN: I am more than willing to help you build the Erie Canal. I'll even give you some money for the project.

CLINTON: I'll accept your offer because building the locks is expensive, but locks are essential because they are the heart of the canal system.

VAN: There is one condition. The locks must be cast iron.

CLINTON: Cast iron? Where on earth can we get cast iron locks?

VAN: Why from my company, and it will only cost you ten million dollars.

CLINTON: Ten million (FIGURES BY PRETENDING TO USE AN ABACUS) Why that's more than the cost of the entire canal! Get out of here, you crook. (CHASES VAN OFF). That's just the kind of help we don't want. We'll have to convince the people that they need the canal, and they'll have to raise the money.

So I went on a tour, and some of the people cheered the idea because it would bring jobs and commerce to the area and open up the West (GIVES DIRECTIONS WHILE MOVING TO THE FRONT OF

	THE AUDIENCE STAGE RIGHT) Now, this half of the audience cheers on my signal.
DESENTER:	DeSenter and others hissed because they feared their taxes would get higher. (CLINTON HAS DESENTER LEAD THE THE HISSING AND BOOING AS LONG AS NEEDED. HE MIMES COLLECTING MONEY)
CLINTON:	There was finally enough money to make a start. On July 4th, 1817, a crowd gathered in Rome, NY, for the groundbreaking ceremonies. To re-create that moment in history, we'll need all of your help. We need to have people cheering and others being a big brass band. But first, we'll need a judge (GET A MEMBER OF AUDIENCE TO BE THE JUDGE) The judge took two spadefuls of dirt - dig, dig, and at that moment, the brass band played (ACTOR #2 DIVIDES THE AUDIENCE IN HALF. ONE-HALF CHEERS AND THE OTHER HALF IMITATES A BRASS BAND. IT MAY REQUIRE ACTOR #2 TO EXPLAIN THE INSTRUMENTS IN A BRASS BAND, BUT SOME MAY HAVE THE ACTUAL TRAINING AND CAN MIME VARIOUS INSTRUMENTS. THE ENTIRE GROUP CAN BE THE BOOMING CANNONS. CLINTON CAN GUIDE THE GROUP BY

Learn Thru Play

RAISING AND LOWERING HIS ARMS TO BUILD TO A CRESCENDO)

CLINTON: The men worked about three months that first summer but only finished fifteen miles. (HE DOES THE MATH ON HIS MIMED ABACUS) At that rate, it will take about twenty-four years to complete the canal, and the people will surely lose interest. Oooh, what am I going to do?

DESENTER: Clinton's folly, look at that! Only fifteen miles in three months. That's the slowest digging I've ever seen. You'll fail; I told you so.

CLINTON: Oooh, she's right. I've got a tremendous problem. We must have professional diggers who only want to work on the canal, but where will I find people like that in a woodcutting and farming area in central New York State?

NEWSBOY: Extra, extra. Get your paper and read the latest news.

CLINTON: (AS VARIOUS PEOPLE) What news? What news? What news?

NEWSBOY: You'll have to buy a paper to find out, mister.

CLINTON: Oh, all right. Fresh kid. (READING MAY BE MIMED OR HAVE A PROP NEWSPAPER) Wow. Listen to this: 1,700 Irish immigrants will arrive in New

	York City. (SNAPS FINGERS) That's it; I'll go to New York and get Irish immigrants. New York City, here I come. "Give my regards to Broadway, remember me to Herald Square," (SINGING PUBLIC DOMAIN SONGS) "East side, West side, all around the town." Here I am at the Port of New York. There's a strong-looking fellow over there. You there, what's your name?
SLUICE:	Sluice McGates. I've just arrived from Ireland and am ready to work.
CLINTON:	And what did you do in Ireland?
SLUICE:	I dug potatoes.
CLINTON:	How would you like a job digging - six days a week from sunrise to sunset? For room and board and fifty cents a day?
SLUICE:	Mr., you got yourself a worker. (THEY SHAKE HANDS) What do you want me to do?
CLINTON:	First, we must clear the land of brush, trees, and roots. We need a path forty feet wide.
SLUICE:	I can't manage all that alone.
CLINTON:	I have all these helpers for you. We need all of you to be workers on the Erie Canal and help Sluice clear the forty foot wide path. Will you show us how to do it,

Sluice? (SLUICE MOVES TO GUIDE THE AUDIENCE)

SLUICE: Sure, first, ya take your axe in your hand (ADD SAFETY COMMENT IF NEEDED) and chop down the trees. Try to get a nice, easy rhythm. We'll use a little ditty to help the work go faster: 1, 2, 3; - 1, 2, 3; cut and clear for the new Erie. (GUIDES AUDIENCE - IT IS POSSIBLE TO USE A FEW MEMBERS FOR EACH TASK OR TO HAVE THE ENTIRE AUDIENCE DO THE ERIE CHANT WHILE THE ACTORS MIME THE BUSINESS)

CLINTON: That's a great team you have working for you. Now, how about clearing the underbrush?

SLUICE: Plowing out the brush will be much faster. You must imagine your hands are a giant cutting blade on a huge plow, and we'll clear the brush. We'll use the same chant with a slight variation of 1, 2, 3; - 1, 2, 3 plow and clear for the new Erie. (GUIDES AUDIENCE)

CLINTON: Well, you've cleared the land. Now, first, you have to dig a 363-mile, four-foot-deep ditch. Do you think you and your workers can do it?

SLUICE: Sure. We'll use this chant,

Learn Thru Play

1, 2, 3; - 1, 2, 3,

dig, dig dig

for the new Erie.

(HE GUIDES THEM THROUGH A FEW REPETITIONS OF THE CHANT/SONG)

CLINTON: Wow, look at that ditch. You and your crew have done it: a great day and a great ditch. But, of course, not everyone thought so. DeSenter always seems to be around

DESENTER: It's a ditch, all right, Clinton's ditch. You'll never get water into it. Never! (LAUGHS) The ditch will leak, and you'll flood the entire countryside.

CLINTON: She's probably right, but I won't know if don't try. I need Sluice to yell off the water level so everyone will know when it looks dangerous. Sluice, can you open the gates? As the water rises, you can close them if the level gets too high.

SLUICE: O.K.

CLINTON: Sluice slowly opened the gates to let the water from a nearby lake fill the canal. Now, I need the first three rows to be the sluice gates, and the rest of you will echo the water level so the countryside will know if there will be a flood.

Learn Thru Play

(GUIDES GROUP THROUGH THE ECHO ACTION. THEY ECHO WHATEVER SLUICE SAYS)

SLUICE: One foot and rising. (AUDIENCE ECHOES)

CLINTON: A little higher Sluice.

SLUICE: Foot and a half. (AUDIENCE ECHOS)

SLUICE: At the three-quarters mark. (AUDIENCE ECHOS)

SLUICE: Three feet and all's well. (AUDIENCE ECHOS)

SLUICE: Four feet. (AUDIENCE ECHOS)

SLUICE: Shut off. Close the gates she's holding.

CLINTON: A cheer went up among the crowd. (GUIDES AUDIENCE THROUGH A CHEER) And as the crowd dispersed, who should have been by Clinton's side but DeSenter?

DESENTER: I didn't think you could do it. Imagine four feet of water in that ditch. But now, how will you get the boats down it?

CLINTON: Easily. We'll have a mule driver walk his mules on the towpath, which runs along the side of the canal. The mules will have a rope hitched to the boat and will pull the boat along.

DESENTER: You mean someone is going to walk his mules along the side of the canal while the mules pull the boat? Who are you going to get for that job? (EXITS)

SLUICE: I'll do it, Mr. Clinton. I don't mind being alone at work because I like to sing, which makes time pass quickly.

CLINTON: Why don't you teach all our future towpath drivers one of your work songs? (GUIDES THE AUDIENCE THROUGH THE ERIE CANAL - MULE VERSE) Thanks, Sluice; oh, by the way, how fast did the mules travel? (THIS MAY BE EXPANDED OR SHORTENED. THE SONG IS WELL KNOWN AND IN THE PUBLIC DOMAIN)

SLUICE: About four miles an hour. We'll lose time when we have to go through a lock.

CLINTON: I better explain a lock. (THIS MAY BE SPOKEN OF OR VISUALLY DEMONSTRATED BY USING AUDIENCE MEMBERS AS SHOWN BELOW OR THROUGH THE UTILIZATION OF SIMPLE PROPS. THIS WILL DEPEND ON THE AGES OF THE AUDIENCE) A lock makes it possible to float boats over hills to travel from one height to another. It's complex so I'll have to show you. We'll need a small boat (SIX MEMBERS OF THE

AUDIENCE) and two lock gates at each end. (FOUR MEMBERS OF THE AUDIENCE) Since the boat is going from a lower to a higher level, the rear lock gauge will be lower than the front lock gates. (GUIDES A BOAT INTO A LOCK) Ready Sluice to open the gates and let the water in?

SLUICE: Right. First three rows, you're the sluice gates, open slowly.

CLINTON: When I give the signal, the rest of you chant, rising higher on the Erie. (HE LEADS CHANT RISING HIGHER, RISING HIGER, RISING HIRE AS THE BOAT RISES)

SLUICE: Level and ready to go.

CLINTON: The packet boat is now even with the surface above, and the boat is ready to go on. The front lock opens, the mules are re-hooked to the boat, and the boat continues. (CLINTON THANKS EVERYONE IN THE AUDIENCE) Thank you, Sluice, for your help.

SLUICE: Well, thank you for all the steady employment. I appreciate the opportunity, Mr. Clinton.

CLINTON: You've got to hand it to the immigrants from all countries who helped to build America. (THE INVOLVEMENT PIECE

Learn Thru Play

MAY END HERE, BUT IF TIME PERMITS, THE FOLLOWING MAY BE USED. THE AUDIENCE MAY BE TAUGHT THE SONG AS AN INTRODUCTION TO THE ENTIRE PLAY OR AT THIS POINT IN THE SHOW).

(DESENTER HURRYS ON)

DESENTER: You may have succeeded regarding the cargo, but what about the passengers? You got a bunch of bridges crossing the canal. They're so low that the passengers are consistently hitting their heads. Some even fall into the canal.

CLINTON: We've developed a song for the boatman to sing to remind the passengers there is a low bridge coming ahead. (TO AUDIENCE) Why don't you join in?

Low bridge, everybody down

Low bridge, yeah, we're coming to a town

And you'll always know your neighbor

And you'll always know your pal

If ya ever navigated on the Erie Canal.

Learn Thru Play

Thank you for helping us build 363 miles of canal from Albany to Buffalo, New York. Give yourselves a big hand.

Learn Thru Play

Movie In The Making

An Involvement Play For Four Actors.

The cast of characters:

ACTOR #1:   Harper, A Hollywood director

ACTOR #2:   Rock Bound, the hero

ACTOR #3:   Bow-Legged, the villain

ACTOR #4:   Rita Book, the heroine

                    (ACTORS #2, #3, & #4 ENTER SINGING AND IN DANCE FORMATION CALIFORNIA, HERE WE COME, RIGHT BACK WHERE...)

HARPER: (ENTERING IN FRONT OF THEM, BLOWS A WHISTLE AND SPEAKS THROUGH A SMALL MEGAPHONE) Cut. (BOTH OR ONE OF THESE PROPS MAY BE USED AS A CONTROL DEVICE WITH THE ADDITION OF THE WORD CUT)

                    Hello, I'm Harper Hollywood, director of motion pictures, movies, cartoons, TV specials, etc.; I just flew in from California to film my latest movie right here in (name Town, City, and State of the current location). Since I only brought a few of my leading actors, the supporting cast will be made up of all of you in, Town, City, and State. (SAID EXACTLY AS SPOKEN ABOVE)

Now, before we begin, there are certain things about making a movie that you should know. The first one is that the director is always in charge. If a scene isn't going well, the director blows a whistle and yells cut, and everyone freezes quietly in place and waits for instructions. To show you how this works, our leading actors will give you a brief demonstration.

ACTORS: (#2, #3, & #4: SING A PUBLIC DOMAIN COWBOY SONG WITH A LOT OF MOVEMENT UNTIL HARPER BLOWS THE WHISTLE AND YELLS THE WORD CUT) Cut. (ACTORS FREEZE IN POSITION) They can't move or talk even if I tell jokes; I'll try one. (TO THE AUDIENCE) Where does the Lone Ranger take the garbage? (CHOOSE A MEMBER OF THE AUDIENCE TO RESPOND TO THIS OLD JOKE. THEN HARPER MUST BLOW THE WHISTLE AND SAY FREEZE) The answer is to'da'dump, to' da'dump, to' 'da'dump, dum, dump. (TO THE TUNE OF THE WILLIAM TELL OVERTURE, THE ACTORS DO NOT

RESPOND TO THIS RATHER WEAK JOKE) See, they didn't laugh. Then, this is how I unfreeze them. (CLAPS TWICE AND ACTORS UNFREEZE)

Now. (TO ACTORS) Let's see if our supporting cast understands. Actors, you can check them to see if we have some talent here. Are you ready? O.K., now, everyone wiggles around, and when I blow the whistle and yell, cut, you freeze. Action. Roll 'em. (AUDIENCE MOVES AND FREEZES) Cut. That was terrific!

We'll begin the movie if you all move back to make a larger acting area.

(AUDIENCE MOVES BACK WITH GUIDANCE FROM THE ACTORS. THERE SHOULD BE AN OPEN FRONT AREA LARGE ENOUGH FOR THE "BUILDING OF THE TOWN" SEQUENCE. THE THREE ACTORS GO BACKSTAGE AFTER THIS IS DONE)

HARPER: We're ready to film our early twentieth-century melodrama. Over 100 years ago, audiences used to get involved in the action at the local theatres and would yell at the actors. There were specific sounds they made for certain characters, and since we need an old-time audience, I'll teach you the sounds.

The first sound is hiss boo. Let's try that. (GUIDES THE AUDIENCE THROUGH HISS BOOS) Good, but try it again a little louder, and we'll see who appears. (AUDIENCE HISS BOOS MORE LOUDLY AND BOW LEGGED APPEARS) Whenever Bow Legged, the villain appears, you all hiss boo.

Most melodramas had a heroine. The heroine of our film is the school marm, Rita Book, and when she appears, you will all sigh ahhh. (HIGH PITCH SOUND) Let's try that, HARPER COMMENTS ON THE LEVEL OF INVOLVEMENT OF THE AUDIENCE. PRAISES THEM FOR A GOOD JOB OR GUIDES THEM TO BE BETTER. IT IS IMPORTANT TO CAPTURE THEIR INTEREST EARLY ON. IF THEY AREN'T INVOLVED AT THE BEGINNING, IT IS PERFECTLY FINE TO CAJOUL THEM WITH HUMOR) Ahhh, ahhh. (RITA ENTERS)

Our next character is Rock Bound; whenever you hear his name, you will cheer. Let's hear you cheer as loudly as you can by saying Yeaahhh! Good. Try that again when I introduce Rock Bound. And now Rock Bound Yeaahhh! the sheriff. (HE APPEARS)

That was excellent. There's one more thing we want you to remember the hand gesture for each character. Hold your hands together when you Yeaahhh! The hero, Rock Bound. (DEMONSTRATES THIS AND GUIDES THE AUDIENCE THROUGH THE ACTION AS THE ACTORS TAKE THE STAGE)

Place your hand over your heart for the heroine, Rita Book, (DOES THE ACTION AS SHE GUIDES THE AAHH) and thumbs down for the villain, Bow Legged. (ACTION AS SHE GUIDES THE HISS BOO)

I can see everyone is ready, so now we can start filming. Places everyone.

The story takes place in a small western town called Tumbledown. This small town. (ROCK BOUND CALLS THE DIRECTOR ASIDE AND STAGE WHISPERS THAT THEY FORGOT TO BRING THE SET)

ROCK: I think you forgot something.

HARPER: (LOOKS SHEEPISH AND LAUGHS IN EMBARRASSMENT) Ha, hah. I seem to have forgotten the set. (AS IF SUDDENLY GETTING AN IDEA). Well, no matter. We'll use some of you to make one side of Main Street. Let's see, I need a bank, a sheriff's office, a general store, a barber shop with a striped pole, and a saloon where thirsty travelers can get a quick buttermilk. The saloon should have swinging doors. (HARPER SETS THIS UP BY PICKING PARTICIPANTS FROM THE AUDIENCE FOR EACH BUILDING. THE OTHER THREE ACTORS HELP WITH THE SETUP AD-LIBBING AS NEEDED)

HARPER: Now, whenever I mention any of the buildings by name, the building mentioned must stand up until the action in that building is completed. Then wait for my direction to sit down. Let's try that. (DIRECTOR RUNS THROUGH THE BUILDINGS SWITCHING ORDER TO KEEP THE "BUILDINGS" ALERT) Thank you. Now, if you'll sit down right where you are, we'll finish casting the play.

BOW LEGGED: Hey Harper. I need thirty vicious desperados to ride with me.

HARPER: Thirty? I'll give you two.

BOW LEGGED: Ten.

HARPER: Three.

BOW LEGGED: Eight?

HARPER: Four is my final offer.

BOW LEGGED: O.K., I need four actors who can look tough. (BOW LEGGED PICKS FROM THE AUDIENCE. HIS CHOICES ARE BASED ON THE TOUGH FACIAL EXPRESSIONS OF THE AUDIENCE VOLUNTEERS. HE TAKES THEM OFF STAGE. HE WALKS WITH BOWED LEGS AND A SWAGGER, AND THE DESPERADOS WILL USUALLY MIMIC HIS WALK)

ROCK: Wait a minute. If he gets four desperados, I need half as many, so two for my posse.

HARPER: O.K. (ROCK PICKS TWO FOR THE POSSE AND TAKES THEM TO HIS OFFICE FOR A BRIEFING)

Well, that's about it. Oops, I almost forgot the sound effects. Whenever you aren't involved in the action, you are to help with the sound effects. The sound of horses' hooves is made by slapping your hands against your legs quickly. (DOES ACTION) The church clock - bong, bong, bong. (DEPENDING ON WHAT TIME THE ACTUAL TIME IS). And whenever the door to the saloon swings open, you'll make the sound of swinging doors opening and closing. (SWISH SWISH) Now, we're ready.

HARPER: It was two o'clock (CHURCH BELLS RING) on an average day in the town of

Tumbledown when suddenly Bow Legged (HISS BOO) and his band of desperados rode into town (HORSES HOOVES) and pulled up in front of the local saloon. They dismounted and entered the saloon (SWISH SWISH) for a quick buttermilk. The schoolmarm, Rita Book, (AAAH) was leaving the General Store. (GESTURES UP STORE) She skipped by the bank, (GESTURES UP BANK) where the bankers were busy counting their money. She went by the sheriff's office, where she waved to Rock Bound, (YEAH! GESTURES UP OFFICE) and Rock Bound came out and waved. She arrived at the barber shop (GESTURES UP BARBER SHOP AND POLE) just as Bow Legged and his band of desperados were leaving the saloon. (SWISH SWISH) She jumped behind the barber pole and overheard their plan to rob the bank. (BOW LEGGED AD-LIBS HIS PLAN) Quietly, she ran past the country store (GESTURES UP STORE) and Barber Shop (GESTURES UP BARBER SHOP) to the sheriff's office, (GESTURES UP OFFICE) where she screamed (AHH) to the sheriff, Rock Bound. (YEAH. HE RUNS OUT)

(WHEN THE ACTORS ARE FINISHED PERFORMING IN FRONT OF A BUILDING AND PROCEED TO THE

Learn Thru Play

NEXT, THE DIRECTOR WILL GUIDE THE PREVIOUS BUILDING TO SIT DOWN)

RITA: Help. They're going to rob the bank.

HARPER: The sheriff came storming out of his office. The desperados, seeing him, leaped on their horses and dashed out of town. (HOOVES) The sound of hooves was loud. Rock Bound (YEAH) gathered his posse and followed. (CHASE SEQUENCE HERE)

HARPER: Cut and print. Now, all the buildings can return to the audience when I unfreeze you, and we'll continue with the next scene. (CLAPS HANDS AND BUILDINGS RETURN TO THE AUDIENCE) Bow Legged (HISS BOO) decided to double back to town and convince Rita Book (AHHHH) to marry him and escape to Mexico.

We'll start the scene with the heroine Rita Book (AHHHH) and Bow Legged. (HISS- BOO) Roll'em, cameras, action. (THIS SCENE IS STYLED AS A MOVIE MELODRAMA)

BOW LEGGED: Rita Book (AHHHH) I've watched you from afar, and you are the girl for me

RITA: Begone, you vile villain. My heart belongs to Sheriff Rock Bound.

BOW LEGGED: If I can't have you, then no one will. The railroad tracks for you. (THEY STAGE A "ROUTINE" OF TYING RITA TO THE TRACKS. WHEN BOWLEGGED HOLDS HER LEGS FLAT, THE UPPER HALF OF HER BODY IS IN A SITTING POSITION. WHEN HE PUSHES THE UPPER HALF DOWN HER LEGS, GO TO A 90-DEGREE ANGLE. THIS CONTINUES THREE TIMES

HARPER: Rock Bound (YEAH) returns to town and hears Rita Book's cries for help.

RITA: Help, help, I'm tied to the railroad tracks.

HARPER: Rock Bound (YEAH) and his posse rode rapidly (HOOVES) to confront Bow Legged (HISS BOO) for a fight to the finish. At that moment, the train chugged to the edge of town. Quick, I need a train. (OPTION OF PICKING INDIVIDUALS OR ANY SIZE GROUP) Follow me!

(AS THE TRAIN IS FOLLOWING HARPER, THE SHERIFF PICKS RITA BOOK OFF THE TRACKS IN THE NICK OF TIME. HE GRABS BOWLEGGED BY THE ARM)

SHERIFF: It's the jail for you, forever.

BOW LEGGED: Curses, foiled again.

HARPER: Cut and print that, and thank you for helping us make our Hollywood Spectacular.

Finale

The preceding pages serve as a guide and catalyst for your own ideas. The examples of successful children's games that focus on getting a class out of their seats and involved in their education may be adapted and expanded to all ages and groups of varying sizes and situations.

The Games Section began in the '70s as a homework assignment in a university setting. Students were to create six games in five chosen academic subjects to assist in the education process of a future academic classroom. These games were to be submitted on 8.5" x 11" copier paper (it would have been ditto paper) in 4" x 6" index card-sized rectangles. These detailed games were formatted this way for future distribution to the entire class. In this manner, individual students obtained copies of everyone's games and were able to create their own card files for future use. Not unlike my mother's recipe file, one could rename, change categories, and file by a means best suited to individual needs. Over the years, my own file would be enhanced and culled until it is the size of the Games section of this text.

My love for puppetry began in a fourth-grade public school class when Miss Atkinson discovered our individual strengths and worked toward them. She must have sensed my flair for the dramatic because I remember making puppets and creating historical plays based on many visits to the library. It wasn't until the puppetry course I took in graduate school that I developed any construction and sewing techniques, which I eventually passed on to my college classes.

The plays and the stage "business" in the included scripts may be adapted and expanded upon. Working in this style is an evolving experience. Comedy requires committed actors, a live audience, and a director who understands the basic rules of comedy, such as: hold for a laugh, never walk on a laugh line, etc.

University students and alumni have successfully performed these plays in front of live audiences of varying ages. Some have created touring companies and enhanced audience interest in more timely issue-based themes. Live theatre is an ongoing learning experience, and as the technique evolved for the actors, it also assisted my understanding of various styles of comedy and how one could involve and excite any age audience. Many more scripted plays are in my teaching and directing arsenal, but they await a separate book.

Enjoy your journey.

Please address questions to:

> Lucha-Burns, LLC
> Attn.: Carol Lucha-Burns
> PO Box 10,
> Whitefield, NH 03598-0010.

About the Author

Carol Lucha-Burns is an award-winning author, playwright, teacher, performer, and director who has been involved in over 200 works of artistic creation. As a Professor of Theatre at the University of New Hampshire, she developed programs in Musical Theatre, Educational Theatre, Storytelling, Directing the Musical, and Puppetry. Although much of her work is centered in New England, where she won the New Hampshire Theatre Conference Lifetime Achievement Award and the New England Theatre Conference Award for Excellence in Theatre Education, she has also taught, written, designed, performed, and directed in Delaware, New York, Pennsylvania, Utah, Syracuse, Manhattan, and Internationally in Tokyo and Vietnam.

Learn Thru Play: Creative Activities That Build Attention, Curiosity, and Collaboration draws on her knowledge of various subjects and student abilities. Like the eclectic family in *Georgia, A New York Story*, her first work of fiction, Carol believes creativity, honesty, standing up for your beliefs, and humor are essential tools of creativity and survival in an ever-changing world.

Her Choice Award-winning reference book, *Musical Notes*, now available on the web as *Musical Notes N' More*, is a valuable resource for those interested in Musical Theatre.

About the Artist

Anniella Pettingill is a multi-faceted creator from Vermont with a long history and love for art.

Previously, she designed posters and the current logo for Elan Academy of Classical Ballet and has been doing freelance commission work for 5+ years. While a student at Pratt Munson, she received the Outstanding First-Year Award and the Easton Pribble Memorial Award in her sophomore year, named after a retired Pratt Munson faculty member and given to the outstanding overall student. As a communications design major, she employs the fundamentals of both graphic design and illustration in her work. Though design work in the modern age calls for a digitized process and outcome, she enjoys working in physical mediums when possible and appropriate, having a penchant for painting, pencils, and inks. Recently, her design was chosen as the official logo for the 50th Anniversary of America's Greatest Heart Run & Walk, associated with the American Heart Association.

www.ingramcontent.com/pod-product-compliance
Lightning Source LLC
LaVergne TN
LVHW051557070426
835507LV00021B/2625